Donna Wilson's

35 Knitted

ANIMALS

AND OTHER CREATURES

Donna Wilson's

35 Knitted ANIMALS

AND OTHER CREATURES

35 UNIQUE AND QUIRKY PATTERNS TO CREATE

CICO BOOKS

LONDON NEW YORK

Published in 2016 by Cico Books,
an imprint of Ryland, Peters & Small Ltd
341 E 116th St, New York, NY, 10029
20-21 Jockey's Fields, London, WC1R 4BW

First published in 2009 under the title *The Knitted Odd-Bod Bunch*

www.rylandpeters.com

10 9 8 7 6 5 4 3 2 1

A CIP catalog record for this book is available from the Library of Congress and the British Library.

ISBN: 978-1-78249-341-9

Printed in China

Editor: Kate Haxell
Designer: Luis Peral-Aranda
Photographer: Geoff Dann
Stylist: Donna Wilson
Illustrator: Luise Roberts

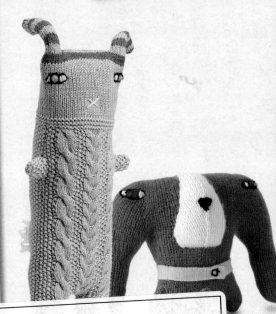

Contents

Introduction

Inspired as they are by the everyday oddities of life, I like to think of each of my creations as a character in my very own wonderland, a place where scale and perception are there to be played with. I love the naivety of children's drawings and the idea that everyone has their quirks. So Harry Hairy Head has a big head and small body, and he likes to groom his hairy head. Peggy Long Legs has extremely long legs, which keep growing as she gets older!

What will happen to you today in Donna's World? You could hang out with Humphrey Hare, pamper a poodle, escape to the woods with the Squirrel-Fox family, or simply have a nibble on a giant, fat-free cupcake!

Especially for this book, my characters have been interpreted into hand knit patterns. This has enabled me to explore knitting techniques that lend themselves to each character, techniques that have given them each a new twist that I love.

Novice knitters will find projects such as Sleepy Pom (page 36) and Percival Long Dog (page 91) very achievable as they just involve a bit of shaping—see instructions for that on pages 118–119 if you need them. Sock knitters will love Oscar Dog (page 41), Fifi Flamingo (page 79), and Stick Snail (page 51), who are some of the creatures that are knitted in the round. If you like cable knitting, then try your hand at Vanessa Hare (page 60), while bead-knitting fans will want to make Deirdre Dragonfly (page 100). For color enthusiasts there are Fair Isle designs including Mitten Kitten (page 69) and Aggie Bear (page 44), plus simpler striped knits, such as Evel Bee (page 74) and Ginge Marmalade (page 13).

I hope you like my creatures—maybe they will remind you of some of your friends! Enjoy knitting them and feel free to send a picture of your new knitted friend to info@donnawilson.com, where I will add some of them to my picture gallery.

Donna Wilson

A note on yarns: I have divided the yarns used into four different categories, which cover the following yarn weights:
Superfine weight: Lace (2 ply)
Fine-weight: Fingering (4 ply)
Lightweight: Sport, Light worsted (DK)
Medium-weight: Worsted (Aran)
Heavyweight: Super-bulky (super-chunky)

The exact weight, ball weight, yardage, and composition of the suggested yarns are given in Yarn Information, on page 126.

Charlie Monkey is always hanging around! He once climbed the Eiffel Tower in Paris without ropes! His hobbies are eating high-energy food and drinking banana milkshakes, going to the gym to strengthen his upper body muscles, and talking to himself—especially when concentrating.

Charlie Monkey

pattern

Note: two strands of Rowan Scottish Tweed are used together throughout to even out the variable weight of the tweed yarn.

FRONT and BACK (both alike)
First leg
*Using the thumb method and A, cast on 5 sts.
Row 1 (RS): Knit.
Row 2: P1, M1L, p3, M1R, p1. (7 sts)
Row 3: K1, M1R, k5, M1L, k1. (9 sts)
Row 4: P1, M1L, p7, M1R, p1. (11 sts)
Row 5: Knit.
Row 6: Purl.
Starting with a k row, work 74 rows st st.*
Cut yarn and put sts onto stitch holder.

Second leg
Work as for First Leg from * to *.
Leave sts on needle and do not cut yarn.

Join legs
Row 81: Knit across 11 sts on needles, cast on 3 sts using the backward loop method, knit across 11 sts from stitch holder. (25 sts)
Row 82: P10, p2tog, p1, p2togtbl, p10. (23 sts)

Body
Starting with a k row, work 62 rows st st.

Shape cheeks
Row 145: K1, M1R, k21, M1L, k1. (25 sts)
Row 146: P1, M1L, p23, M1R, p1. (27 sts)
Row 147: K1, M1R, k25, M1L, k1. (29 sts)
Row 148: Purl.

Row 149: Knit.
Row 150: Purl.
Row 151: K1, skpo, k23, k2tog, k1. (27 sts)
Row 152: P1, p2tog, p21, p2togtbl, p1. (25 sts)
Row 153: K1, skpo, k19, k2tog, k1. (23 sts)
Starting with a p row, work 11 rows st st.
Row 165: K1, skpo, k17, k2tog, k1. (21 sts)
Row 166: Purl.
Row 167: K1, skpo, k15, k2tog, k1. (19 sts)
Row 168: Purl.
Row 169: K1, skpo, k13, k2tog, k1. (17 sts)
Row 170: P1, p2tog, p11, p2togtbl, p1. (15 sts)
Bind (cast) off.

ARMS (make two)
Using the thumb method and A, cast on 13 sts.
Row 1: Knit.
Row 2: Purl.
Starting with a k row, work 86 rows st st.
Row 89: [K2, k2tog] three times, k1. (10 sts)
Row 90: Purl.
Row 91: [K1, k2tog] three times, k1. (7 sts)
Row 92: [P2tog] three times, k1. (4 sts)
Cut yarn leaving a long tail. Pass yarn through rem 4 sts, pull up tight and secure end.

TAIL
Work as for Arms.

Size
Completed creature measures approx. 20in (50cm) tall

Yarn suggestion
Fine-weight yarn such as Rowan Scottish Tweed 4 ply (used double) 4 x 1oz (25g) balls in A (gray—Lewis Gray 00007)
Lightweight yarn (such as Debbie Bliss Baby Cashmerino) 1 x 1³⁄₄oz (50g) ball in B (pink—340016)

Needles
Pair of US 4 (3.5mm) knitting needles

Extras
One stitch holder
Tapestry needle
Washable toy filling
Oddments of black, blue, and white tapestry wool for embroidery

Gauge (Tension)
18 sts and 34 rows to 4in (10cm) over st st using US 4 (3.5mm) needles

Abbreviations
See page 126

NOSE

Using the thumb method and B, cast on 7 sts.

Row 1: Knit.
Row 2: P1, M1L, p5, M1R, p1. (9 sts)
Row 3: K1, M1R, k7, M1L, k1. (11 sts)
Row 4: Purl.
Row 5: K1, M1R, k9, M1L, k1. (13 sts)
Starting with a p row, work 3 rows st st.
Row 9: K1, M1R, k11, M1L, k1. (15 sts)
Row 10: P1, M1L, p13, M1R, p1. (17 sts)
Row 11: Knit.
Row 12: P1, M1L, p15, M1R, p1. (19 sts)
Starting with a k row, work 3 rows st st.
Row 16: P1, p2tog, p13, p2togtbl, p1. (17 sts)
Row 17: Knit.
Row 18: P1, p2tog, p11, p2togtbl, p1. (15 sts)
Row 19: K1, skpo, k9, k2tog, k1. (13 sts)
Starting with a p row, work 3 rows st st.
Row 23: K1, skpo, k7, k2tog, k1. (11 sts)
Row 24: Purl.
Row 25: K1, skpo, k5, k2tog, k1. (9 sts)
Row 26: P1, p2tog, p3, p2togtbl, p1. (7 sts)
Bind (cast) off.

FINISHING

Press pieces gently following directions on the yarn wrapper.
Note that the arms and tail are not stuffed.
Pin nose to center of face, following photograph for position. Thread a tapestry needle with yarn B and using mattress stitch, sew around edge of nose to attach it to face. Before completing sewing, insert toy filling in nose.
Pin arms to edges of front body approx. 6in (15cm) from top of head. Using mattress stitch, sew body pieces together around outer edges, catching arms into seam, weaving loose ends into the seam wherever possible, and leaving a small opening. Insert toy filling and sew opening closed.
Sew the tail to the back, centered just above the legs.

Embroider as follows:
The face: for each eye, using black tapestry wool and backstitch, embroider an oval with a vertical line either side of the iris area. Fill in the irises with satin stitch in blue and the areas on either side with satin stitch in white; for the eyebrows, using black and backstitch, embroider a short line above each eye; for the mouth, using black and backstitch, embroider a horizontal line on the nose. See also page 124.

Harry is one of a kind: he eats fluff for lunch and always loves being brushed and groomed. He is well known for his hairy head and sometimes makes people around him sneeze.

Harry Hairy Head

pattern

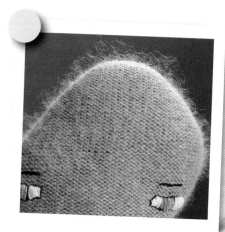

Note: two strands of Kid Classic are used together for Head, one from each ball.

FRONT and BACK BODY (both alike)
First leg
*Using US 1 (2.50mm) needles, the cable method, and A, cast on 10 sts.
Row 1 (RS): Knit.
Row 2: Purl.
Row 3: K2, M1R, k to last 2 sts, M1L, k2. (12 sts)
Row 4: Purl.
Rep rows 3–4 once more. (14 sts)
Row 7: Knit.
Row 8: Purl.*
Cut yarn, put sts onto stitch holder.
Second leg
Work as for First Leg from * to *.
Leave sts on needle and do not cut yarn.
Join legs
Knit across 14 sts on needle, cast on 10 sts, knit across 14 sts from stitch holder. (38 sts)
Body
Starting with a p row, work 19 rows st st,
Shape arms
Next row: K2, M1R, k to last 2 sts, M1L, k2. (40 sts)
Next row: Purl.
Rep last 2 rows once more. (42 sts)
Next row: Knit.
Next row: Cast on 8 sts, p to end. (50 sts)
Next row: Cast on 8 sts, k to end. (58 sts)
Next row: Purl.

Next row: K2, M1R, k to last 2 sts, M1L, k2. (60 sts)
Next row: Purl.
Rep last 2 rows once more. (62 sts)
Next row: Knit.
Next row: Purl.
Rep last 2 rows once more.
Next row: K2, skpo, k to last 4 sts, k2tog, k2. (60 sts)
Next row: Purl.
Rep last 2 rows once more. (58 sts)
Next row: Knit.
Next row: Bind (cast) off 10 sts, p to end. (48 sts)
Next row: Bind (cast) off 10 sts, k to end. (38 sts)
Next row: Purl.
Next row: Knit.
Put sts onto holder.
Block and press both pieces on holders.

HEAD
With WS of one body piece facing and using two ends of B, purl 25 sts from holder onto first US 6 (4mm) double-pointed needle. Purl rem 13 sts onto second double-pointed needle. With WS of second body piece facing, purl 13 sts onto second double-pointed needle, purl final 25 sts onto third double-pointed needle. (76 sts)
Keeping WS of body facing outwards, use fourth needle to work in the round.
Knit three rounds, thus establishing

Size
Completed creature measures approx. 15$\frac{1}{4}$in (38cm) tall
Yarn suggestion
Lightweight yarn (such as Rowan Cotton Glacé) 1 x 1$\frac{3}{4}$oz (50g) ball in A (green—Ivy 812)
Medium-weight mohair yarn (such as Rowan Kid Classic) 2 x 1$\frac{3}{4}$oz (50g) balls in B (lilac—Lavender Ice 841)
Needles
Pair of US 1 (2.5mm) knitting needles
Set of four double-pointed US 6 (4mm) knitting needles
Extras
Two stitch holders
Two round markers
Tapestry needle
Washable toy filling
Oddments of black, green, and white tapestry wool for embroidery
Gauge (Tension)
21 sts and 30 rows to 4in (10cm) over rev st st using two ends of B and US 6 (4mm) needles
Abbreviations
See page 126

rev st st on RS of work, and cont work on WS of head.

Place round marker before first and 39th sts.

Next round: *K1, k2tog, k to 3 sts before marker, skpo, k1, rep from * once more. (72 sts)

Knit 1 round.

Rep last two rounds three more times. (60 sts)

Knit 7 rounds.

Next round: K to 1 st before marker, M1, k2, M1, k to end. (62 sts)

Knit 1 round.

Rep last 2 rounds once more. (64 sts)

Next round: K1, M1, k to 1 st before marker, M1, k2, M1, k to last st, M1, k1. (68 sts)

Knit 1 round.

Rep last 2 rounds once more. (72 sts)

Next round: K to 1 st before marker, M1, k2, M1, k to end. (74 sts)

Knit 1 round.

Rep last 2 rounds six more times. (86 sts)

Knit 9 rounds.

Next round: K2, k2tog, k to last 4 sts, skpo, k2. (84 sts)

Rep last round four more times. (76 sts)

Knit 1 round.

Next round: *K1, k2tog, k to 3 sts before marker, skpo, k1, rep from * once more. (72 sts)

Rep last 2 rounds nine more times. (36 sts)

Next round: *K1, k2tog, k to 3 sts before marker, skpo, k1, rep from * once more. (32 sts)

Rep last round four more times. (16 sts)

Rearrange sts so there are 8 sts on each of first and second needles.

Bind (cast) off all sts, casting off 1 st from each needle together.

FINISHING

Weave in all loose ends.

Turn creature inside out so RS (rev st st) side of head is outermost. Roll up a cotton dishtowel and place it inside head as a former, then steam head gently.

Using mattress stitch, sew body pieces together around outer edges from neck to underarm. Insert toy filling into head and arms through open legs, then sew up leg seams, inserting toy filling in legs as you sew seam.

Embroider as follows:

The face: for each eye, using black tapestry wool and backstitch, embroider an oval with a vertical line either side of the iris area. Fill in the irises with satin stitch in green and the areas on either side with satin stitch in white; for the eyebrows, using black and backstitch, embroider a line above each eye; for the mouth, using black and backstitch, embroider an oval opening and outline the teeth. Fill in the teeth with satin stitch in white. See also page 124.

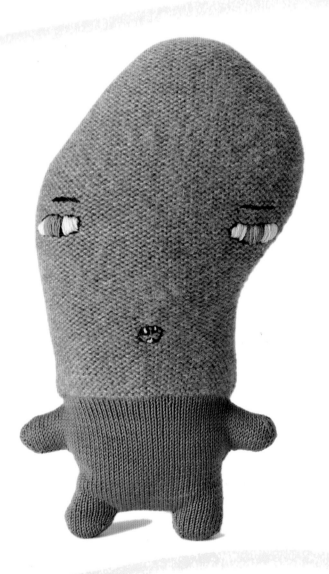

Ginge Marmalade

Ginge is a pure-bred marmalade cat.
During the day he doesn't do much
apart from eat and sleep, but at night he
gets up to all sorts of fun. He has held
the record for singing on a tightrope
while holding a pint of milk with his tail!

pattern

FRONT

First leg

*Using the thumb method and A, cast on
3 sts.

Row 1 (RS): Knit.

Row 2: P1, M1L, p1, M1R, p1. (5 sts)
Join in B.

Row 3: Using B, k1, M1R, k3, M1L, k1.
(7 sts)

Row 4: Using B, purl.
The last 4 rows form the st st stripe patt, rep
throughout. Strand the yarn not in use on
the WS up the right-hand edge. Work
shaping as follows:

Row 5: K1, M1R, k5, M1L, k1. (9 sts)
Starting with a p row, work 5 rows st st.*
Cut yarns and put sts onto stitch holder.

Second and third legs

Work as for First Leg.

Fourth leg

Work as for First Leg from * to *.
Leave sts on needle and do not cut yarns.

Join legs

Keeping the stripe patt correct:

Row 11: Knit across 9 sts of the Fourth Leg,
[cast on 2 sts using the backward loop
method, with RS facing, knit across 9 sts of
the next Leg on stitch holder] three times.
(42 sts)

Body

Row 12: P8, [p2togtbl, p2tog, p7] twice,
p2tog, p2togtbl, p8. (36 sts)
Starting with a k row, work 6 rows st st,
ending after 2 rows using A.

Row 19: Using B, k1, skpo, k to end.
(35 sts)
Starting with a p row, work 3 rows st st.

Row 23: Using B, k1, skpo, k to end.
(34 sts)

Row 24: Purl.

Row 25: Using A, k1, skpo, k to end. (33 sts)

Row 26: Purl.

Row 27: Using B, k1, skpo, k to end. (32 sts)

Row 28: Purl.

Row 29: Using A, k1, skpo, k to end. (31 sts)

Row 30: Purl.

Row 31: Using B, k1, skpo, k to end. (30 sts)

Row 32: Purl.

Row 33: Using A, k1, skpo, k to end. (29 sts)
Starting with a p row, work 3 rows st st.

Row 37: Using A, k1, skpo, k to end. (28 sts)
Starting with a p row, work 5 rows st st.

Row 43: Using B, k1, skpo, k to last 3 sts,
k2tog, k1. (26 sts)
Starting with a p row, work 7 rows st st.

Row 51: Using B, k1, skpo, k to end. (25 sts)
Starting with a p row, work 9 rows st st.

Row 61: Using A, k1, skpo, k to end. (24 sts)
Starting with a p row, work 9 rows st st,
ending after 2 rows using A.

Shape first ear

Row 71: K8, turn.
Work on this set of 8 sts only and put the
rem sts on a stitch holder.

Row 72: P1, p2tog, p to end. (7 sts)

Row 73: K to last 3 sts, k2tog, k1. (6 sts)
Rep rows 72–73 twice more. (2 sts)
Bind (cast) off and cut yarns.

Shape second ear

Put the 16 sts from stitch holder onto
needle, with RS facing rejoin yarn.

Row 71: Bind (cast) off 8 sts, k to end.
(8 sts).

Row 72: P to last 3 sts, p2togtbl, p1.
(7 sts)

Row 73: K1, skpo, k to end. (6 sts)
Rep rows 72–73 twice more. (2 sts)
Bind (cast) off and cut yarns.

BACK

Work as given for Front, reversing RS of work (to make a mirrored pair of pieces) by reading knit for purl and vice versa. See page 118 for reverse shaping tips.

TAIL

Using the thumb method and A, cast on 12 sts.

Row 1 (RS): Knit.

Row 2: Purl.

Join in B.

Row 3: Knit.

Row 4: Purl.

The last 4 rows form the st st stripe patt, rep throughout. Strand the yarn not in use on the WS up the right-hand edge.

Starting with a k row, work 112 rows in st st, ending after 2 rows using B.

Row 117: Using A, [k2, k2tog] three times. (9 sts)

Row 118: Using A, purl.

Cut A.

Row 119: Using B, [k1, k2tog] three times. (6 sts)

Row 120: Using B, [p2tog] three times. (3 sts)

Cut yarn leaving a long tail. Pass yarn through rem 3 sts, pull up tight and secure.

FINISHING

Press pieces gently following directions on the yarn wrapper.

Note that the tail is not stuffed.

Using mattress stitch, sew row ends of tail together, leaving cast-on end open.

Position tail at the bottom of decrease edge on front body. Using mattress stitch, sew body pieces together around the outer edge, catching tail into seam, weaving loose

ends into the seam wherever possible, and leaving a small opening. Insert toy filling and sew opening closed.

Embroider as follows:

The face: for each eye, using black tapestry wool and backstitch, embroider an oval with a vertical line either side of the iris area. Fill in the irises with satin stitch in green and the areas on either side with satin stitch in white; for the nose and mouth, using black and backstitch, embroider an inverted triangle with a vertical line descending from the apex to touch the top of a second triangle; for the whiskers, using white make fringe loops (as you would for the ends of a scarf) under stitches on each cheek. See also page 124.

Neerg's favorite food is grass. He used to be a white bunny, but since he started eating grass his fur has changed color permanently.

Neerg Green Bunny

pattern

FRONT and BACK (both alike)

First leg

*Using the thumb method and A, cast on 5 sts.

Row 1 (WS): Purl.

Row 2: K1, M1R, k3, M1L, k1. (7 sts)

Row 3: P1 [k1, yarn forward between the needles, sl1, yarn back between the needles] rep to last 2 sts, k1, p1.

Row 4: Knit.

Row 5: As row 3.

Rows 6–7: Rep rows 4–5.

Row 8: K1, M1R, k5, M1L, k1. (9 sts)

Row 9: P1 [yarn forward between the needles, sl1, yarn back between the needles k1] rep to last 2 sts, yarn forward between the needles, sl1, p1.

Row 10: Knit.

Row 11: As row 9.*

Cut yarn and put sts onto stitch holder.

Second leg

Work as for First Leg from * to *.

Cut yarn and leave sts on needle.

Join legs

Join in B.

Row 12 (RS): Knit across 9 sts on needle, cast on 20 sts using the backward loop method, knit across 9 sts from stitch holder. (38 sts)

Row 13: P8, p2tog, p18, p2togtbl, p8. (36 sts)

Row 14: Knit.

Row 15: Purl.

Starting with a k row, work 20 rows st st.

Shape arms

Row 36: K1, M1R, k to last st, M1L, k1. (38 sts)

Row 37: P1, M1L, p to last st, M1R, p1. (40 sts)

Rep rows 36–37 twice more. (48 sts)

Starting with a k row, work 2 rows st st.

Row 44: K1, skpo, k to last 3 sts, k2tog, k1. (46 sts)

Row 45: P1, p2tog, p to last 3 sts, p2togtbl, p1. (44 sts)

Rep rows 44–45 twice more. (36 sts)

Starting with a k row, work 10 rows st st.

Shape first ear

Row 60: K9, turn.

Work on this set of 9 sts only and put the rem stitches onto a stitch holder.

**Starting with a p row, work 15 rows st st.

Row 76: K1, skpo, k3, k2tog, k1. (7 sts)

Row 77: Purl.

Bind (cast) off as follows: k1, skpo, pass the first st loop on the right-hand needle over the second, k1, pass the first st loop on the right-hand needle over the second, k2tog, pass the first st loop on the right-hand needle over the second, k1, pass the first st loop on the right-hand needle over the second.

Fasten off.**

Shape second ear

Put next 9 sts on stitch holder onto needle, rejoin yarn with RS facing, k9, turn,

Rep from ** to **.

Shape third ear

Work as for Second Ear.

Shape fourth ear

Work as for Second Ear.

Size

Completed creature measures approx. 8in (20cm) tall

Yarn suggestion

Lightweight yarn (such as Rowan Wool Cotton) small amount in A (green—Elf 946) and 1 x 1³/₄oz (50g) ball in B (acid green—Citron 901)

Fine-weight yarn (such as Rowan Pure Wool 4 ply) small amount in C (cream—Snow 412)

Needles

Pair of US 3 (3.25mm) knitting needles

Extras

One stitch holder

Tapestry needle

Washable toy filling

Oddments of black, green, white, and pink tapestry wool for embroidery

Gauge (Tension)

26 sts and 36 rows to 4in (10cm) over st st using US 3 (3.25mm) needles

Abbreviations

See page 126

FINISHING

Press pieces gently following directions on the yarn wrapper.

Using mattress stitch, sew body pieces together around the outer edges, leaving a small opening. Insert toy filling and sew opening closed.

Using C, make a small pompom and attach to back of the body.

Embroider as follows:

The face: for each eye, using black tapestry wool and backstitch, embroider an oval with a vertical line either side of the iris area. Fill in the irises with satin stitch in green and the areas on either side with satin stitch in white; for each mouth, using pink, embroider a cross. See also page 124.

Size

Completed creature measures approx. 7in (18cm) tall

Yarn suggestion

Lightweight yarn (such as Rowan Cotton Glacé) 1 x 1³/₄oz (50g) ball in A (sand—Ochre 833) and 1 ball in B (red—Poppy 741)

Needles

Pair of US 2 (3mm) knitting needles

Set of four double-pointed US 2 (3mm) knitting needles

Extras

Tapestry needle

Washable toy filling

Oddments of black, brown, white, and red tapestry wool for embroidery

Gauge (Tension)

28 sts and 42 rows to 4in (10cm) over st st using US 2 (3mm) needles

Abbreviations

See page 126

Stripy Head is one of the smallest in the world of the creatures. He loves hiding from people and popping out in the most unexpected places. He is fond of jam sandwiches and dislikes seafood.

Stripy Head

pattern

ARMS (make four)

Using US 2 (3mm) needles, the thumb method, and A, cast on 5 sts.

Row 1 (RS): Using A, knit.

Row 2: Using A, purl.

Join in B.

Row 3: Using B, knit.

Row 4: Using B, purl.

Cut A and B 4in (10cm) from last st on needle, put sts onto a double-pointed needle.

FRONT and BACK BODY (both alike)

First leg

Using US 2 (3mm) needles, the thumb method, and A, cast on 5 sts.

Row 1 (RS): Using A, knit.

Row 2: Using A, purl.

Join in B.

Row 3: Using B, k to last st, M1L, k1. (6 sts)

Row 4: Using B, purl.

The last 4 rows form the stripe st st patt, rep throughout. Strand the yarn not in use on the WS up the right-hand edge. Work as follows:

Starting with a k row, work 4 rows st st.

Cut A and B 4in (10cm) from last st on needle, put sts onto a double-pointed needle.

Second leg

Using US 2 (3mm) needles, the thumb method, and A, cast on 5 sts.

Row 1 (RS): Using A, knit.

Row 2: Using A, purl.

Join in B.

Row 3: Using B, k1, M1R, k to end. (6 sts)

Row 4: Using B, purl.

Starting with a k row, work 4 rows in stripe st st patt.

Do not cut yarn.

Join legs

Keeping the stripe patt correct.

Row 9: Using A, knit across 6 sts on needle, cast on 4 sts using the backward loop method, with RS facing, knit across 6 sts from double-pointed needle. (16 sts)

Row 10: Using A, p5, p2tog, p2, p2togtbl, p5. (14 sts)

Row 11: Using B, knit.

Row 12: Using B, p1, p2tog, p to last 3 sts, p2togtbl, p1. (12 sts)

Starting with a k row, work 3 rows in stripe st st patt.

Row 16: Using B, p1, p2tog, p to last 3 sts, p2togtbl, p1. (10 sts)

Starting with a k row, work 8 rows in stripe st st patt.

Cut A and B 4in (10cm) from last st on needle.

Join in arms

Row 25: Using A and RS facing, k5 sts of one arm piece, cast on 3 sts using the backward loop method, k10 sts of the body section, cast on 3 sts using the backward loop method, k5 sts of a second arm piece. (26 sts)

Row 26: Using A, p1, [p2tog, p1] twice, p2togtbl, p8, p2tog, [p1, p2togtbl] twice, p1. (20 sts).

Row 27: Using B, knit.

Row 28: Using B, p1, p2tog, p to last 3 sts, p2togtbl, p1. (18 sts)

Row 29: Using A, knit.

Row 30: Using A, p1, p2tog, p to last 3 sts, p2togtbl, p1. (16 sts)

Rep rows 27–30 once more. (12 sts)

Cut A and B 4in (10cm) from last st on needle, put sts onto a double-pointed needle.

HEAD

Select one Front/Back piece as the Back. Starting with this piece RS facing, arrange the stitches on three US 2 (3mm) double-pointed needles as follows:

Slip the left 6 sts from the Back and the following 2 sts from the Front onto a third needle, slip 8 sts from the Front onto a fourth needle and slip the rem 2 sts on the front needle onto the back needle. Place a round marker at the center back. (8 sts on each needle)

Join in B at the center back.

Rounds 1–2: Using B, knit.

Join in A, Cont to work in stripe patt, twisting the yarns together at each color change and stranding the color not in use on the WS.

Rounds 3–4: Using A, knit.

Rep rounds 1–2 once more.

Round 7: Using A, knit.

Round 8: Using A, k1, M1R, k6, M1L, k1 on each needle. (10 sts on each needle)

Knit 3 rounds in stripe patt set.

Round 12: Using A, k1, M1R, k8, M1L, k1 on each needle. (12 sts on each needle)

Knit 3 rounds in stripe patt set.

Round 16: Using A, k1, M1R, k10, M1L, k1 on each needle. (14 sts on each needle)

Knit 3 rounds in stripe patt set.

Round 20: Using A, k1, M1R, k12, M1L, k1 on each needle. (16 sts on each needle)

Knit 3 rounds in stripe patt set.

Round 24: Using A, k1, M1R, k14, M1L, k1 each needle. (18 sts on each needle)

Knit 19 rounds in stripe patt set.

Round 44: Using A, k1, skpo, k3, k2tog, k2, skpo, k3, k2tog, k1 on each needle. (14 sts on each needle)

Cut A and cont in B.

Round 45: K1, skpo, k1, k2tog, k2, skpo, k1, k2tog, k1 on each needle. (10 sts on each needle)

Round 46: K1, [skpo, k2tog] twice, k1 on each needle. (6 sts on each needle)

Round 47: K1, skpo, k2tog, k1 on each needle. (4 sts on each needle)

Round 48: K1, k2tog, k1 on each needle. (3 sts on each needle)

Cut B 4in (10cm) from the last stitch on the needle and thread into a tapestry needle. Pass the tapestry needle through all the stitches on the needles in the order they would have been knitted, use the tip of the needle to pull the yarn at the point just after it has passed through the first stitch to draw the stitches tight to the yarn, then pull the yarn tight as it emerges through the last stitch. Secure the end.

FINISHING

Press pieces gently following directions on the yarn wrapper.

Using mattress stitch, sew body pieces together around the outer edges, weaving loose ends into seam wherever possible, and leaving a small opening. Insert toy filling and sew opening closed.

Embroider as follows:

The face: for each eye, using black tapestry wool and backstitch, embroider an oval with a vertical line either side of the iris area. Fill in the irises with satin stitch in brown and the areas on either side with satin stitch in white; for the eyebrows, using black and backstitch, embroider a short, slanting line above each eye; for the mouth, using black and backstitch, embroider a small oval and fill this in with satin stitch in red. See also page 124.

Beryl the Bold

Beryl is a dog-cat: she's definitely a dog, but traces of cat have been found in her ancestry. She always got teased at school for this, but now she's happy with who she is! She loves chocolate chip ice cream and going on short walks. She's sometimes a bit moody but always says sorry if she's snapped at anyone.

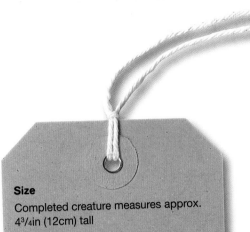

Size

Completed creature measures approx. 4¾in (12cm) tall

Yarn suggestion

Lightweight yarn (such as Rowan Wool Cotton) 1 x 1¾oz (50g) ball in A (cream—Antique 900) and 1 ball in B (light brown—Dream 929)

Needles

Pair of US 2 (3mm) knitting needles

Extras

Two stitch holders or large safety pins

Tapestry needle

Washable toy filling

Oddments of black, green, and white tapestry wool for embroidery

½ x 8in (1 x 20cm) of pink craft felt

Small bell

Gauge (Tension)

23 sts and 32 rows to 4in (10cm) over st st using US 2 (3mm) needles

Abbreviations

See page 126

pattern

FRONT

Back leg

Using the thumb method and A, cast on 3 sts.

Row 1 (RS): Knit.
Row 2: P1, M1L, p1, M1R, p1. (5 sts)
Row 3: Knit.
Row 4: Purl.
Rep rows 3–4 once more.
Row 7: Knit.
Row 8: P4, M1R, p1. (6 sts)
Cut yarn and put sts onto a stitch holder.

Second leg

Using the thumb method and A, cast on 3 sts.

Row 1: Knit.
Row 2: P1, M1L, p1, M1R, p1. (5 sts)
Starting with a k row, work 5 rows st st.
Row 8: P1, M1L, p3, M1R, p1. (7 sts)
Cut yarn and put sts onto a stitch holder.

Third and fourth legs

Work as for Second Leg.

Join legs

Row 9: Cast on 17 sts, knit across 7 sts of fourth leg, cast on 3 sts using the backward loop method, with RS facing, knit across 7 sts of the third leg, cast on 18 sts using the backward loop method, knit across 7 sts of the second leg, cast on 3 sts using the backward loop method, knit across 6 sts of the back leg. (68 sts)

Shape body

Row 10: P5, p2tog, p1, p2togtbl, p5, p2tog, p16, p2togtbl, p5, p2tog, p1, p2togtbl, p5, p2tog, p16.
(61 sts)
Join in B.
Starting with a knit (RS) row and using a separate length of yarn for each block of color, twisting the colors together on the WS to avoid holes forming, work color patt from the chart. Work shaping as follows:
Row 11: K1, M1R, k to end. (62 sts)
Row 12: P to last st, M1R, p1. (63 sts)

Rows 13–18: Rep rows 11–12 three times. (69 sts)
Row 19: K1, M1R, k to end. (70 sts)
Row 20: Purl.
Rows 21–26: Rep rows 19–20 three times. (73 sts)
Row 27: Knit.
Row 28: Purl.
Row 29: K1, M1R, k to end. (74 sts)

Head

Row 30: P7, put the last 7 sts onto a stitch holder, bind (cast) off 35 sts, p to end.
Work on this set of 32 sts only for the head.
Row 31: K to last 3 sts, k2tog, k1. (31 sts)
Row 32: P1, p2tog, p to end. (30 sts)
Row 33: K1, M1R, k to last 3 sts, k2tog, k1. (30 sts)
Row 34: P1, p2tog, p to end. (29 sts)
Row 35: Knit.
Rows 36–39: Rep rows 34–35 twice. (27 sts)
Row 40: Purl.
Row 41: Knit.
Row 42: Purl.

Shape first ear

Row 43: K6, put the last 6 sts onto a stitch holder, bind (cast) off 15 sts, k5.
Cut B and cont work using A.
Work on this set of 6 sts only for the first ear.
Row 44: P3, p2togtbl, p1. (5 sts)
Row 45: K1, skpo, k2. (4 sts)
Row 46: P1, p2togtbl, p1. (3 sts)
Bind (cast) off.

Shape second ear

Put sts on second stitch holder onto needle and with WS facing rejoin A.
Row 44: P1, p2tog, p3. (5 sts)
Row 45: K2, k2tog, k1. (4 sts)
Row 46: P1, p2tog, p1. (3 sts)
Bind (cast) off.

Tail

Put sts on first stitch holder onto needle and with the RS facing rejoin A.
Row 31: K1, skpo, k4. (6 sts)
Row 32: P3, p2togtbl, p1. (5 sts)

Cut A and join in B.
Row 33: Knit.
Row 34: P2, p2togtbl, p1. (4 sts)
Rows 35–39: Starting with a k row, work
5 rows st st.
Row 40: P2tog, p2togtbl. (2 sts)
Bind (cast) off.

BACK

Work as given for Front, reversing RS of
work (to make a mirrored pair of pieces) by
reading knit for purl and vice versa. See
page 118 for reverse shaping tips.

FINISHING

Press pieces gently following directions on
the yarn wrapper.
Using mattress stitch; sew the body pieces
together around the outer edges, weaving
loose ends into seam wherever possible,
and leaving a small opening. Insert toy filling
and sew opening closed.
Embroider as follows:
The face: for each eye, using black tapestry
wool and backstitch, embroider an oval with
a vertical line either side of the iris area. Fill
in the irises with satin stitch in green and the
areas on either side with satin stitch in white;
for the nose, using black and satin stitch,

embroider an inverted triangle with a vertical
line of backstitch descending from the apex;
for the mouth, using black and backstitch,
embroider a circular opening and outline the
teeth. Fill in the teeth with satin stitch in white.
See also page 124.
Cut the felt to fit around Beryl's neck, sew
on the bell, and sew the ends of the collar
together around her neck.

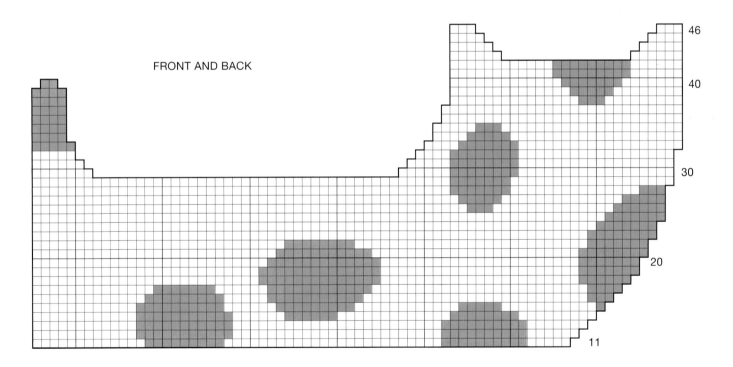

FRONT AND BACK

A

B

Tig is Beryl and Ginge's only child and is their pride and joy, Tig was named after her great-grandfather, Tigger, who was a very famous actor. She is small and cuddly and loves everything pink.

Little Tig

pattern

Note: one length of yarn A is used for the body with shorter lengths of yarn B worked together with yarn A for the spots as indicated on the chart.

FRONT
Front leg
*Using the thumb method and A, cast on 5 sts.
Row 1 (WS): Purl.
Row 2: K1, M1R, k3, M1L, k1. (7 sts)
Starting with a p row, work 3 rows st st.
Row 6: K1, M1R, k5, M1L, k1. (9 sts)
Starting with a p row, work 3 rows st st.
Row 10: K8, M1L, k1. (10 sts)
Row 11: Purl.*
Cut yarn and put sts onto stitch holder.

Back leg
Using A and B stranded together, work as for First Leg from * to *.
Leave sts on needle and do not cut yarn.

Join legs
Row 12: Using A and B stranded together, knit across 10 sts on needle, cast on 4 sts using the backward loop method, using A only and RS facing, knit across 10 sts from stitch holder, cast on 22 sts using the backward loop method. (46 sts)

Body
Row 13: P21, p2togtbl, p8, p2tog, using A and B together p2, p2togtbl, p9. (43 sts)
Starting with a knit (RS) row and using a separate length of B for each block of A and B color indicated, work color patt from the chart. Work shaping as follows:
Row 14: K to last st, M1L, k1. (44 sts)
Row 15: P1, M1L, p to end. (45 sts)
Rows 16–19: Rep rows 14–15 twice. (49 sts)
Row 20: Knit.
Row 21: P1, M1L, p to end. (50 sts)
Rows 22–25: Rep rows 20–21 twice. (52 sts)
Rows 26–28: Starting with a k row, work 3 rows st st.
Row 29: P1, M1L, p to end. (53 sts)
Rows 30–32: Starting with a k row, work 3 rows st st.
Row 33: P1, M1L, p to end. (54 sts)
Rows 34–53: Starting with a k row, work 20 rows st st.
Row 54: K1, skpo, k to end. (53 sts)
Row 55: Purl.
Rows 56–57: Rep rows 54–55 once. (52 sts)
Row 58: K1, skpo, k to end. (51 sts)
Row 59: P to last 3 sts, p2togtbl, p1. (50 sts)
Row 60: K1, skpo, pass the k st over the dec st, k to end. (48 sts)
Row 61: Purl.

Shape first ear
Row 62: Bind (cast) off 11 sts, k10, put the last 11 sts onto a stitch holder, bind off 15 sts, k10.
Cut B and cont in A.
Work on this set of 11 sts only for the first ear.

Size
Completed creature measures approx. 7¹/₂in (19cm) tall

Yarn suggestion
Lightweight yarn (such as Rowan Pure Wool DK) 2 x 1³/₄oz (50g) balls in A (pink—Tea Rose 025) and 1 ball in C (dark pink—Hyacinth 026)
Superfine-weight yarn (such as Rowan Kidsilk Haze) 1 x 1oz (25g) ball in B (dark pink—Candy Girl 606)

Needles
Pair of US 5 (3.75mm) knitting needles

Extras
One stitch holder
Tapestry needle
Washable toy filling
Oddments of black, pale green, and white tapestry wool for embroidery

Gauge (Tension)
24 sts and 36 rows to 4in (10cm) over st st using A and US 5 (3.75mm) needles

Abbreviations
See page 126

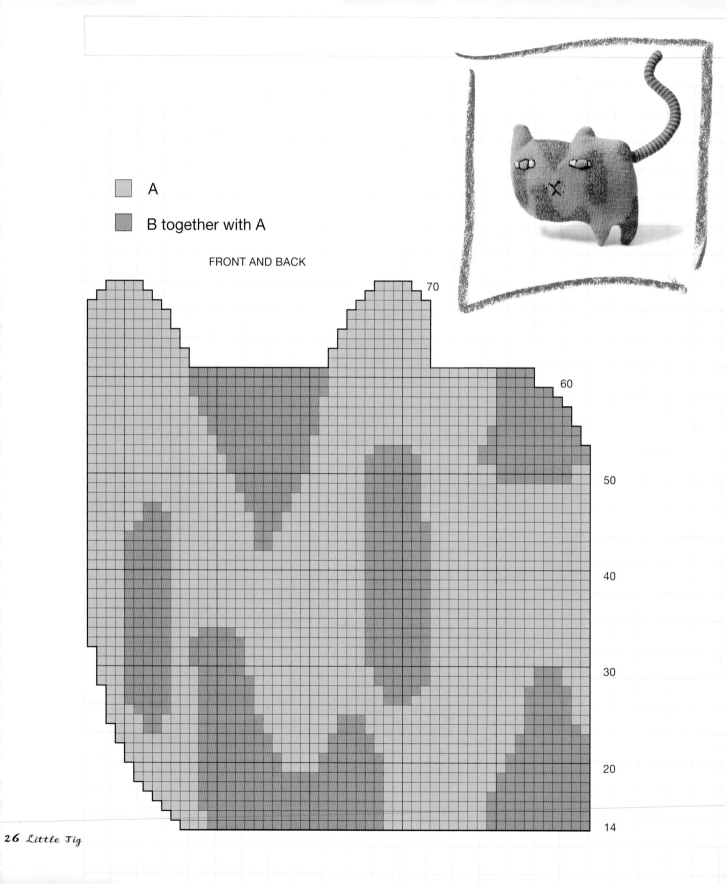

A

B together with A

FRONT AND BACK

70

60

50

40

30

20

14

Row 63: Purl.
Row 64: K1, skpo, k8. (10 sts)
Row 65: Purl.
Row 66: K1, skpo, k7. (9 sts)
Row 67: Purl.
Row 68: K1, skpo, k6. (8 sts)
Row 69: P1, p2tog, p2, p2togtbl, p1. (6 sts)
Row 70: K1, skpo, k2tog, k1. (4 sts)
Bind (cast) off.
Shape second ear
Put 11 sts on stitch holder onto a needle
and with WS facing, rejoin A.
Row 63: Purl.
Row 64: K to last 3 sts, k2tog, k1. (10 sts)
Row 65: Purl.
Row 66: K to last 3 sts, k2tog, k1. (9 sts)
Row 67: Purl.
Row 68: K to last 3 sts, k2tog, k1. (8 sts)
Row 69: P1, p2tog, p2, p2togtbl, p1. (6 sts)
Row 70: K1, skpo, k2tog, k1. (4 sts)
Bind (cast) off.

BACK
Work as given for Front,
reversing RS of work (to make
a mirrored pair of pieces) by reading knit
for purl and vice versa. See page 118 for
reverse shaping tips.

TAIL
Using the thumb method and C, cast on
67 sts.
Row 1: K2C, [k1A, k1C] rep to last 3 sts,
k1A, k2C.
Row 2: P2C, [p1A, p1C] rep to last 3 sts,
p1A, p2C.
Rep rows 1–2 seven more times.
Using C, bind (cast) off.

FINISHING
Press pieces gently following directions on
the yarn wrapper.
Using mattress stitch, sew the body pieces
together around the outer edges, weaving

loose ends into seam wherever possible,
and leaving a small opening. Insert toy filling
and sew opening closed.
Using mattress stitch and C, sew the two
long edges of the tail together by sewing
into the row two rows from the cast-on and
two rows from the bound-off edges and
around and through the stitches worked in C
only. This fills the tail as you seam it. If the
creature is not going to be given to a child,
you can push a length of wire into the tail to
allow you to shape it. Sew tail in position
with seam facing downward.

Embroider as follows:
The face: for each eye, using black tapestry
wool and backstitch, embroider an oval with
a vertical line either side of the iris area. Fill
in the irises with satin stitch in pale green
and the areas on either side with satin stitch
in white; for the nose and mouth, using
black and backstitch, embroider an inverted
triangle with a vertical line descending from
the apex to touch the top of a second
triangle; for the whiskers, using black
embroider small straight stitches on both
cheeks. See also page 124.

Olive Owl may be small but she has a loud voice! People can hear her twit-twoos from ten miles away. Olive loves her home and enjoys housework and gardening. She makes a mean apple pie.

Olive Owl

pattern

FRONT
Using the thumb method and A, cast on 19 sts.
Join in B.
Starting with a knit (RS) row, strand the yarn not in use loosely across WS of work and work color patt from the chart. Work shaping as follows:
Row 1 (RS): Knit.
Row 2: Purl.
Rows 3–16: Starting with a k row, work 14 rows st st.
Row 17: K1, skpo, k13, k2tog, k1. (17 sts)
Rows 18–30: Starting with a p row, work 13 rows st st.
Cut B and cont to work using A.
Shape first ear
Row 31: K4, put these 4 sts onto a stitch holder, bind (cast) off 9 sts, k3.
Work on this set of 4 sts only for the first ear
Row 32: P1, p2togtbl, p1. (3 sts)
Row 33: Knit.
Row 34: P1, p2togtbl. (2 sts)
Row 35: Knit.
Row 36: P2togtbl. (1 st)
Fasten off.
Shape second ear
Put 4 sts from stitch holder onto needle and with the WS facing, rejoin A.
Row 32: P1, p2tog, p1. (3 sts)
Row 33: Knit.
Row 34: P1, p2tog. (2 sts)
Row 35: Knit.

Row 36: P2tog. (1 st)
Fasten off.

BACK
Work as given for Front using A only.

BASE
Using the thumb method and A, cast on 11 sts.
Row 1: Knit.
Row 2: P1, M1L, p9, M1R, p1, (13 sts)
Row 3: K1, M1R, k11, M1L, k1, (15 sts)
Row 4: P1, M1L, p13, M1R, p1, (17 sts)
Starting with a k row, work 2 rows st st.
Row 7: K1, skpo, k11, k2tog, k1, (15 sts)
Row 8: P1, p2tog, p9, p2togtbl, p1, (13 sts)
Row 9: K1, skpo, k7, k2tog, k1, (11 sts)
Bind (cast) off.

WING PIECE ONE (make two)
Using the thumb method and A, cast on 5 sts.
Row 1: Knit.
Row 2: P1, M1L, p3, M1R, p1, (7 sts)
Row 3: K1, M1R, k5, M1L, k1, (9 sts)
Row 4: P8, M1R, p1, (10 sts)
Row 5: K1, M1R, k9, (11 sts)
Row 6: P10, M1R, p1, (12 sts)
Row 7: K1, M1R, k11, (13 sts)
Row 8: P10, p2togtbl, p1, (12 sts)
Row 9: Bind (cast) off 3 sts, k5, k2tog, k1, (8 sts)
Bind (cast) off.

Size
Completed creature measures approx. 5¹⁄₂in (14cm) tall
Yarn suggestion
Lightweight yarn (such as Rowan Pure Wool DK) 1 x 1¾oz (50g) ball in A (pink—Sugar Pink 038) and 1 ball in B (orange—Quarry 035)
Needles
Pair of US 6 (4mm) knitting needles
Extras
One stitch holder
Tapestry needle
Washable toy filling
Oddments of black and gray tapestry wool for embroidery
Gauge (Tension)
22 sts and 30 rows to 4in (10cm) over st st using US 6 (4mm) needles
Abbreviations
See page 126

WING PIECE TWO (make two)

Using the thumb method and A, cast on
5 sts.
Row 1: Purl.
Row 2: K1, M1R, k3, M1L, k1, (7 sts)
Row 3: P1, M1L, p5, M1R, p1, (9 sts)
Row 4: K8, M1L, K1, (10 sts)
Row 5: P1, M1L, p9, (11 sts)
Row 6: K10, M1L, k1, (12 sts)
Row 7: P1, M1L, p11, (13 sts)
Row 8: K10, k2tog, k1, (12 sts)
Row 9: Bind (cast) off 3 sts, p5, p2togtbl,
p1, (8 sts)
Bind (cast) off.

FINISHING

Press pieces gently following directions on
the yarn wrapper.
Using mattress stitch sew the body pieces
together around the outer edges, leaving the
cast-on edges open. Sew the base to the
cast-on edges, weaving the loose ends into
the seam wherever possible, and leaving a
small opening. Insert toy filling and sew
opening closed.
Using mattress stitch, sew one of each wing
piece together around the outer edge,
weaving the loose ends into the seam
wherever possible, and leaving a small
opening. Insert toy filling and sew opening
closed. Position the wings on either side
of the body so that the bound-off edge is
facing forward: this means for the left-hand
wing, wing piece two will be uppermost and
for the right-hand wing, wing piece one will
be uppermost.
Embroider as follows:
The face: for each eye, using black tapestry
wool and satin stitch, embroider a circle
with radiating straight stitches; for the
beak, using gray and satin stitch, embroider
a triangle.
The feet: for each foot, using gray tapestry
wool, embroider separate straight stitches
over the bottom of the front body onto the
base. See also page 124.

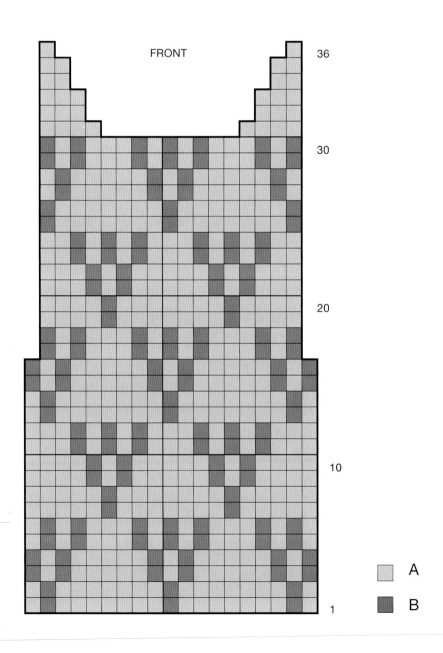

FRONT

36

30

20

10

1

A

B

Terry and Tina Twin are good friends, but I guess they'd
have to be. Terry is calm and easy-going; Tina is small but
feisty and usually gets her way. Terry likes reading and
writing stories; Tina likes robots and dislikes bad breath.

Terry and Tina Twin

pattern

FRONT BODY

First leg

Using US 4 (3.50mm) needles, the thumb method, and A, cast on 5 sts.
*Row 1 (WS): Purl.
Row 2: K1, M1R, k3, M1L, k1. (7 sts)
Row 3: Purl.
Row 4: K1, M1R, k5, M1L, k1. (9 sts)
Row 5: Purl.
Row 6: Knit.
Row 7: Purl.*
Row 8: K1, M1R, k to end. (10 sts)
Row 9: Purl.
Rep rows 8–9 twice more. (12 sts)
Cut yarn and put sts onto a stitch holder.

Second leg

Work as for First Leg from * to *.
Row 8: K to last st, M1L, k1. (10 sts)
Row 9: Purl.
Rep rows 8–9 twice. (12 sts)
Cut yarn and leave sts on the needle.

Join legs

Join in B.
Row 14 (RS): Knit across 12 sts on needle, cast on 22 sts using the backward loop method, with RS facing knit across 12 sts from stitch holder. (46 sts)

Body

Row 15: P11, p2tog, p20, p2togtbl, p11. (44 sts)
Starting with a k row, work 4 rows st st.
Join in C.
Rows 20–25: Work in st st, using C and stranding B up the right-hand edge. (6 rows)
Rows 26–31: Work in st st, using B and stranding C up the right-hand edge. (6 rows)
Rep rows 20–31 three more times, then rep rows 20–25 once more.
Cut C and cont in B.
Starting with a k row, work 2 rows st st.
Row 76: K1, skpo, k to last 3 sts, k2tog, k1. (42 sts)
Row 77: Purl.

Row 78: As row 76. (40 sts)**
Row 79: P24, bind (cast) off 4 sts, p11. (24 sts on one needle. 12 sts on other)
Cut B 4in (10cm) from last st on needle and put sts onto a double-pointed needle.

BACK BODY

Work as for Front Body to **.
Row 79: P12, bind (cast) off 4 sts, p24. (12 sts on one needle, 24 sts on other)
Cut B 4in (10cm) from last st on needle and put sts onto a double-pointed needle.

ARMS

Arm fronts

***Using C, place a slip knot on a US 2 (3mm) needle and with RS facing, pick up 6 sts along one edge of the last (uppermost) stripe of C on front body, cast on 1 st.
Starting with a p row, work 7 rows st st.
Row 8: K1, skpo, k to last 3 sts, k2tog, k1. (5 sts)
Row 9: Purl.
Row 10: K1, skpo, k to last 3 sts, k2tog, k1. (3 sts)
Row 11: Purl.
Bind (cast) off.***
Rep from *** to *** on the other edge of the same stripe.

Arm backs

Work as for Arm Fronts, working on Back Body piece.

SMALLER HEAD

Leave the two sets of 12 sts from the body pieces on separate double-pointed needles, put rem sts onto waste yarn.
Split the sts from the Back Body onto two double-pointed needles. (6 sts on each needle)
Transfer 2 sts from each end of the group of sts from the Front Body onto the neighbor-

ing needle holding sts from the Back Body piece. (8 sts on each of three needles)

With the Back Body piece facing, join in A on the left-hand needle and place round marker at this point.

Round 1: Knit.

Round 2: [K1, skpo, k2, k2tog, k1] three times. (6 sts on each needle)

Knit 5 rounds.

Round 8: [K1, MIR, k to last st on double-pointed needle, MIL, k1] three times. (8 sts on each needle)

Round 9: Knit.

Rep rounds 8–9 three more times. (14 sts on each needle)

Knit 12 rounds.

Round 28: [K1, skpo, k to last 3 sts on double-pointed needle, k2tog, k1] three times. (12 sts on each needle)

Round 29: Knit.

Rep rounds 28–29 once more. (10 sts on each needle)

Rep round 28 twice more. (6 sts on each needle)

Round 34: [K1, skpo, k2tog, k1] three times. (4 sts on each needle)

Round 35: [Skpo, k2tog] three times. (2 sts on each needle)

Cut A 4in (10cm) from the last stitch on the needle and thread into a tapestry needle. Pass the tapestry needle through all the stitches on the needles in the order they would have been knitted, use the tip of the needle to pull the yarn at the point just after it has passed through the first stitch to draw the stitches tight to the yarn, then pull the yarn tight as it emerges through the last stitch. Secure the end.

LARGER HEAD

Place the two sets of 24 sts from the body pieces onto separate double-pointed needles.

Split the sts from the Back Body onto two double-pointed needles.

(12 sts on each needle)

Transfer 4 sts from each end of the group of sts from the Front Body onto the neighboring needle holding sts from the Back Body piece. (16 sts on each of three needles)

With the Back Body piece facing, join in A, on the left-hand needle and place round marker at this point.

Round 1: Knit.

Round 2: [K1, skpo, k10, k2tog, k1] three times. (14 sts on each needle)

Knit 3 rounds.

Round 6: [K1, skpo, k8, k2tog, k1] three times. (12 sts on each needle)

Knit 2 rounds.

Round 9: [K1, MIR, k to last st on double-pointed needle, MIL, k1] three times. (14 sts on each needle)

Knit 3 rounds.

Rep rounds 9–12 once more. (16 sts on each needle)

Round 17: Knit.

Round 18: As round 9. (18 sts on each needle)

Knit 24 rounds.

Round 43: [K1, skpo, k to last 3 sts on double-pointed needle, k2tog, k1] three times. (16 sts on each needle)

Round 44: Knit.

Rep rounds 43–44 once more. (14 sts on each needle)

Round 47: Knit.

Rep round 43 four more times. (6 sts on each needle)

Round 52: [K1, skpo, k2tog, k1] three times. (4 sts on each needle)

Round 53: [Skpo, k2tog] three times. (2 sts on each needle)

As for Smaller Head, cut A 4in (10cm) from the needle, thread into a tapestry needle and pass this through the rem sts, starting with the first st of the round, and draw tight.

FINISHING

Press pieces gently following directions on the yarn wrapper.

Using mattress stitch, sew the body pieces together around the outer edge, weaving loose ends into seam wherever possible, and leaving a small opening. Insert toy filling and sew opening closed.

Embroider as follows:

The faces: for each eye, using black tapestry wool and backstitch, embroider an oval with a vertical line either side of the iris area. Fill in the irises with satin stitch in green and the areas on either side with satin stitch in white; the mouth, using black and satin stitch, embroider a small mouth on each head. See also page 124.

Bunny Blue

Bunny Blue is fond of food, particularly picnics in the back yard. If he can have his favorite raspberry juice to drink, then he's very happy.

pattern

FRONT and BACK (both alike)

First leg

*Using the thumb method and A, cast on 5 sts.

Row 1 (WS): Purl.

Row 2: K1, M1R, k3, M1L, k1. (7 sts)

Row 3: Purl.

Row 4: K1, M1R, k5, M1L, k1. (9 sts)

Row 5: Purl.

Cut A and join in B.

Row 6: Knit.

Row 7: Purl.*

Row 8: K1, M1R, k to end. (10 sts)

Starting with a p row, work 3 rows st st.

Row 12: K1, M1R, k to end. (11 sts)

Row 13: Purl.

Cut yarn and put sts onto a stitch holder.

Second leg

Work as for First Leg from * to *.

Row 8: K to last st, M1L, k1. (10 sts)

Starting with a p row, work 3 rows st st.

Row 12: K to last st, M1L, k1. (11 sts)

Row 13: Purl.

Leave sts on needle and do not cut yarn.

Join legs

Row 14 (RS): Knit across 11 sts on needles, cast on 12 sts using the backward loop method, knit across 11 sts on stitch holder. (34 sts)

Shape body

Row 15: P10, p2tog, p10, p2togtbl, p10. (32 sts)

Starting with a k row, work 16 rows st st.

Shape arms

Row 32: K1, M1R, k to last st, M1L, k1. (34 sts)

Row 33: P1, M1L, p to last st, M1R, p1. (36 sts)

Rep rows 32–33 twice more. (44 sts)

Starting with a k row, work 4 rows st st.

Row 42: K1, skpo, k to last 3 sts, k2tog, k1. (42 sts)

Row 43: P1, p2tog, p to last 3 sts, p2togtbl, p1. (40 sts)

Rep rows 42–43 once more. (36 sts)

Starting with a k row, work 4 rows st st.

Shape first ear

Row 50: K9, turn.

**Work on this set of 9 sts only and put the rem stitches onto a stitch holder.

Starting with a p row, work 21 rows st st.

Row 72: K1, skpo, k3, k2tog, k1. (7 sts)

Row 73: Purl.

Bind (cast) off as follows: k1, skpo, pass the first st loop on the right-hand needle over the second, k1, pass the first st loop on the right-hand needle over the second, k2tog, pass the first st loop on the right-hand needle over the second, k1, pass the first st loop on the right-hand needle over the second.**

Shape second ear

Put next 9 sts on stitch holder onto needle, rejoin yarn with RS facing, k9, turn, Rep from ** to **.

Shape third ear

Work as for Second Ear.

Shape fourth ear

Work as for Second Ear.

FINISHING

Press pieces gently following directions on the yarn wrapper.

Using mattress stitch, sew body pieces together around the outer edges, leaving a small opening. Insert toy filling and sew opening closed.

Using C, make a small pompom and attach to back of body, centered just above legs.

Embroider as follows:

The face: for each eye, using black tapestry wool and backstitch, embroider an oval with a vertical line either side of the iris area. Fill in the irises with satin stitch in blue and the areas on either side with satin stitch in white; for the mouth, using pink, embroider a cross. See also page 124.

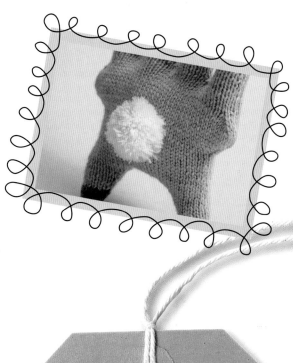

Size

Completed creature measures approx. 6¼in (16cm) tall

Yarn suggestion

Fine-weight yarn (such as Rowan Pure Wool 4 ply) small amount in A (light brown—Hessian 416), 1 x 1¾oz (50g) ball in B (pale blue—Chalk 445), and small amount in C (cream—Snow 412)

Needles

Pair of US 2 (2.75mm) knitting needles

Extras

One stitch holder

Tapestry needle

Washable toy filling

Oddments of black, blue, cream, and pink tapestry wool for embroidery

Gauge (Tension)

33 sts and 44 rows to 4in (10cm) over st st using US 2 (2.75mm) needles

Abbreviations

See page 126

Sleepy Pom is always dozing off—there's nothing he likes more than curling up in bed under his cozy duvet. He even dreams about sleeping!

Sleepy Pom

pattern

FRONT and BACK (both alike)
First leg
*Using the cable method and A, cast on
4 sts.
Row 1 (RS): Knit.
Row 2: Purl.
Row 3: Inc, k1, inc, k1. (6 sts)
Starting with a p row, work 3 rows st st.
Row 7: Inc, k3, inc, k1. (8 sts)
Starting with a p row, work 3 rows st st.
Cut A and join in B.
Cont in garter st (knit every row).
Knit 2 rows.*
Row 13: Inc, k to end. (9 sts)
Knit 5 rows.
Rep last 6 rows twice more. (11 sts)
Knit 2 rows.
Put sts onto stitch holder.
Second leg
Work as for First Leg from * to *.
Row 13: K to last 2 sts, inc, k1. (9 sts)
Knit 5 rows.
Rep last 6 rows twice more. (11 sts)
Knit 2 rows.
Join legs
Next row: Knit across 11 sts on needle, cast on 2 sts, knit across 11 sts on stitch holder. (24 sts)
Shape body
Knit 3 rows.
Next row: Skpo, k to last 2 sts, k2tog. (22 sts)
Knit 7 rows.
Rep last 8 rows twice more. (18 sts)
Knit 8 rows.

Shape arms
Next row: Cast on 7 sts, k to end. (25 sts)
Rep last row once more. (32 sts)
Knit 2 rows.
Next row: Skpo, k to last 2 sts, k2tog. (30 sts)
Knit 1 row.
Rep last 2 rows seven more times. (16 sts)
Shape head
Cut B and join in C.
Next row: Knit.
Next row: Purl.
Next row: Inc, k to last 2 sts, inc, k1. (18 sts)
Next row: Purl.
Rep last 2 rows seven more times. (32 sts)
Starting with a k row, work 4 rows st st.
Next row: Skpo, k to last 2 sts, k2tog.
Next row: P2tog, p to last 2 sts, p2togtbl.
Next row: Skpo, k to last 2 sts, k2tog.
Bind (cast) off.

FINISHING

Do not press knitted pieces. Using mattress stitch, sew body pieces together around the outer edges, weaving loose ends into the seam wherever possible, and leaving a small opening. Insert toy filling and sew opening closed.
Using A, make two pompoms approx. 2in (5cm) in diameter. Sew one pompom to each top corner of head.
Embroider as follows:
The face: for each eye, using black tapestry wool and backstitch, embroider a half-circle; for the mouth, using red, embroider a cross.
See also page 124.

Size
Completed creature measures approx.
12in (30cm) tall
Yarn suggestion
Medium-weight yarn (such as
Lion Brand Vanna's Choice Baby)
1 x 3½oz (100g) ball in
A (pale green—Sweet Pea 169),
1 ball in B (orange—Goldfish 132), and
1 ball in C (mint green—Mint 168)
Needles
Pair of US 5 (3.75mm) knitting needles
Extras
One stitch holder
Tapestry needle
Washable toy filling
Oddments of black and red tapestry wool for embroidery
Gauge (Tension)
20 sts and 30 rows to 4in (10cm) over st st using US 5 (3.75mm) needles
Abbreviations
See page 126

TAIL UPPER

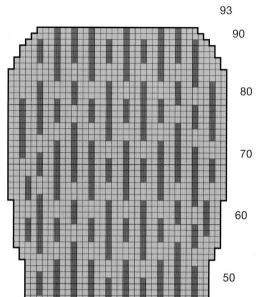

93
90
80
70
60
50
40
30
20
10
1

A
B

Cyril is from fox and squirrel descent. He's always been a keen storyteller and loves an audience to listen to his tales of adventure. He adores traveling and his great-great uncle was an infamous, sly red fox explorer. Cyril is very much in love with Rita Raccoon and they have two offspring—Ralf and Rill.

Cyril Squirrel~Fox

pattern

FRONT and BACK (both alike)
First leg
Using the thumb method and A, cast on 5 sts.
*__Row 1 (WS):__ Purl.
Row 2: K1, M1R, k3, M1L, k1. (7 sts)
Row 3: Purl.
Row 4: Knit.
Row 5: Purl.
Rep rows 4–5 twice more.*
Row 10: K6, M1l, k1. (8 sts)
Row 11: Purl.
Cut yarn and put sts onto stitch holder.
Second leg
Work as for First Leg from * to *.
Row 10: K1 M1R, k6. (8 sts)
Row 11: Purl.
Leave sts on needle and do not cut yarn.
Join legs
Row 12 (RS): Knit across 8 sts on needle, cast on 10 sts using the backward loop method, with RS facing knit across 8 sts from stitch holder. (26 sts)
Body
Row 13: P7, p2tog, p8, p2togtbl, p7. (24 sts)
Starting with a k row, work 40 rows st st.
Shape arms
Row 54: K1, M1R, k to last st, M1L, k1. (26 sts)

Row 55: P1, M1L, p to last st, M1R, p1. (28 sts)
Row 56: K1, M1R, k to last st, M1L, k1. (30 sts)
Starting with a p row, work 4 rows st st.
Row 61: P1, p2tog, p to last 3 sts, p2togtbl, p1. (28 sts)
Row 62: K1, skpo, k to last 3 sts, k2tog, k1. (26 sts)
Row 63: P1, p2tog, p to last 3 sts, p2togtbl, p1. (24 sts)
Head
Starting with a k row, work 22 rows st st.
Shape first ear
Row 86: K12, turn.
Work on this set of 12 sts only and put the rem sts on stitch holder.
Row 87: P1, p2tog, p to end. (11 sts)
Row 88: K to last 3 sts, k2tog, k1. (10 sts)
Rep rows 87–88 three more times. (4 sts)
Row 95: Purl.
Bind (cast) off.
Shape second ear
Put sts on stitch holder onto a needle and with RS facing, rejoin yarn.
Row 86: Knit.
Row 87: P to last 3 sts, p2togtbl, p1. (11 sts)
Row 88: K1, skpo, k to end. (10 sts)

Size

Completed creature measures approx. 8¾in (22cm) tall

Yarn suggestion

Fine-weight yarn (such as Rowan Pure Wool 4 ply) 1 x 1¾oz (50g) ball in A (orange—Spice 434) and 1 ball in B (dark brown—Mocha 417)

Needles

Pair of US 2 (3mm) knitting needles

Extras

One stitch holder

Tapestry needle

Washable toy filling

Oddments of dark brown, green, and white tapestry wool for embroidery

Gauge (Tension)

30 sts and 40 rows to 4in (10cm) over st st using US 2 (3mm) needles

Abbreviations

See page 126

Rep rows 87–88 three more times. (4 sts)
Row 95: Purl.
Bind (cast) off.

TAIL UPPER

Using the thumb method and A, cast on
26 sts.
Join in B.
Starting with a knit (RS) row and stranding
yarn not in use loosely across WS of work,
work color patt from the chart. Work
shaping as follows:
**Rows 1–30: Starting with a k row, work
30 rows st st.
Row 31: K1, M1R, k to last st, M1L, k1.
(28 sts)
Row 32: Purl.
Rows 33–34: Rep rows 31–32 once. (30 sts)
Rows 35–40: Starting with a k row, work
6 rows st st.
Row 41: K1, M1R, k to last st, M1L, k1. (32 sts)
Rows 42–54: Starting with a p row, work
13 rows st st.
Row 55: K1, M1R, k to last st, M1L, k1. (34 sts)
Row 56: Purl.
Rows 57–58: Rep rows 55–56 once. (36 sts)
Rows 59–64: Starting with a k row, work
6 rows st st.
Row 65: K1, M1R, k to last st, M1L, k1.
(38 sts)
Rows 66–86: Starting with a p row, work
21 rows st st.
Row 87: K1, skpo, k to last 3 sts, k2tog, k1.
(36 sts)
Row 88: Purl.
Rows 89–90: Rep rows 87–88 once. (34 sts)
Row 91: K1, skpo, k to last 3 sts, k2tog, k1.
(32 sts)
Row 92: P1, p2tog, p to last 3 sts, p2togtbl,
p1. (30 sts)
Row 93: K1, skpo, k to last 3 sts, k2tog, k1.
(28 sts) **
Cut B. Cont to work using A.
Row 94: [P1, p2tog] twice, [p2tog] eight
times, [p1, p2tog] twice, (16 sts)
Bind (cast) off.

TAIL UNDERSIDE

Using the thumb method and A, cast on
16 sts.
Using A only, work as for written instructions
for Tail Upper from ** to **, deducting 10 sts
from stitch totals given in brackets at the
end of the rows.
Bind (cast) off.

NOSE

Using the thumb method and A, cast on
28 sts.
Row 1 and every alt row (WS): Purl.
Row 2: K24, short-row-wrap the next
st, turn.
Row 4: K20, short-row-wrap the next
st, turn.
Row 6: K16, short-row-wrap the next
st, turn.
Row 8: K12, short-row-wrap the next
st, turn.
Row 10: K8, short-row-wrap the next
st, turn.
Row 12: K4, short-row-wrap the next
st, turn.
Row 14: K4, [pick up the short-row-wrap
and k tog with wrapped st, k3] six times.
Rep rows 1–14, twice.
Bind (cast) off.

FINISHING

Press pieces gently following directions on
the yarn wrapper.
Using mattress stitch, sew cast-on and
bound-off edges of nose together. Insert toy
filling into nose. Using mattress stitch, sew
nose to front of head, following photograph
for position.
Using mattress stitch, sew body pieces
together around the outer edges, weaving
loose ends into the seam wherever possible,
and leaving a small gap. Insert toy filling and
sew opening closed.
Using mattress stitch, sew tail pieces
together around shaped outer edges,
weaving loose ends into the seam wherever
possible. Insert toy filling then sew cast-on
edges to back body, following photograph
for position.
Embroider as follows:
The face: for each eye, using dark brown
tapestry wool and backstitch, embroider an
oval with a vertical line either side of the iris
area. Fill in the irises with satin stitch in
green and the areas on either side with satin
stitch in white; for the nose, using dark
brown and satin stitch, embroider over the
tip of the knitted nose. See also page 124.

Oscar Dog

Oscar is a rare, stripy, sausage dog.
Because he has been blessed with
unusually good hearing, he can hear a
person coming up to ten miles away,
and can sometimes hear what people
are saying in the next room.

Size
Completed creature measures approx. 15¼in (38cm) long

Yarn suggestion
Medium-weight yarn (such as Lion Brand Cotton-Ease) 1 x 3½oz (100g) ball in A (dark gray—Charcoal 152) and 1 ball in B (turquoise—Turquoise 148)

Needles
Set of five double-pointed US 5 (3.75mm) knitting needles

Pair of US 5 (3.75mm) knitting needles

Extras
One round marker

Tapestry needle

Washable toy filling

Oddments of black, blue, and white tapestry wool for embroidery

Gauge (Tension)
21 sts and 34 rows to 4in (10cm) over st st using US 5 (3.75mm) needles

Abbreviations
MB = make bobble. Knit into front and back of next stitch six times, [turn, p6, turn, k6] three times, turn, p6, turn, [k2tog] three times, pass second then first stitch over third stitch

Note: use fifth double-pointed needle to work bobbles

See also page 126

pattern

STRIPE PATTERN
2 rows A.

2 rows B.

Work in stripe patt throughout stranding yarn not in use on WS.

BODY, HEAD, and LEGS
Using US 5 (3.75mm) double-pointed needles, the cable method, and A, cast on 57 sts. Arrange stitches over three needles, make sure stitches are not twisted and use fourth needle to knit first and last stitches together to join into the round. Place round marker at start of round.

Round 1 (RS): Knit. (56 sts)

Shape tail
Round 2: K26, s2tog, k1, psso, k27. (54 sts)

Round 3: K25, s2tog, k1, psso, k26. (52 sts)

Round 4: K20, skpo, k2, s2tog, k1, psso, k2, k2tog, k21. (48 sts)

Round 5: K22, s2tog, k1, psso, k23. (46 sts)

First back leg
Round 6: K19, skpo, s2tog, k1, psso, k2tog, k19, MB. (42 sts)

Round 7: K19, s2tog, k1, psso, k20. (40 sts)

Round 8: K16, skpo, s2tog, k1, psso, k2tog, k17. (36 sts)

Knit 5 rounds.

Second back leg
Round 14: K to last st, MB.

Body
Knit in rounds without shaping until work measures 10in (25cm) from cast-on edge, ending with an A stripe.

Shape head
Next round: Knit.

Next round: K18, M1, k18. (37 sts)

Knit 2 rounds.

Next round: K16, M1L, k5, M1R, k16. (39 sts)

Knit 2 rounds.

Next round: K14, M1L, k3, M1L, k5, M1R, k3, M1R, k14. (43 sts)

Knit 2 rounds.

Next round: K15, M1L, k4, M1L, k5, M1R, k4, M1R, k15. (47 sts)

First front leg
Next round: K to last st, MB.

Next round: K16, M1L, k5, M1L, k5, M1R, k5, M1R, k16. (51 sts)

Knit 5 rounds.

Next round: K21, skpo, k5, k2tog, k21. (49 sts)

Second front leg
Next round: K to last st, MB.

Next round: K20, skpo, k5, k2tog, k20. (47 sts)

Next round: Bind (cast) off 8 sts, k to last 8 sts, bind (cast) off. (31 sts)

Rejoin A to rem sts and work back and forth in rows using US 5 (3.75mm) knitting needles.
Next row: K12, skpo, k3, k2tog, k12. (29 sts)
Next row: P1, p2tog, p to last 3 sts, p2togtbl, p1. (27 sts)
Shape nose
Work 4 rows st st.
Next row: K1, skpo, k8, skpo, k1, k2tog, k8, k2tog, k1. (23 sts)
Work 3 rows st st.
Next row: K1, skpo, k6, skpo, k1, k2tog, k6, k2tog, k1. (19 sts)
Next row: Purl.
Next row: K1, skpo, k4, skpo, k1, k2tog, k4, k2tog, k1. (15 sts)
Next row: Purl.
Next row: K1, skpo, k2, skpo, k1, k2tog, k2, k2tog, k1. (11 sts)
Next row: Purl.
Next row: K1, [skpo] twice, k1, [k2tog] twice, k1. (7 sts)
Cut yarn leaving a long tail. Pass yarn through rem 7 sts and pull up tight.

EARS (both together)
Using US 5 (3.75mm) knitting needles, the thumb method, and A, cast on 10 sts.
Cut A and complete ears in B.
*__Row 1:__ Knit.
Row 2: Sl 1, k to end.
Rep row 2 twenty more times.
Row 23: K2tog, k to last 2 sts, k2tog.
Row 24: Knit.
Rep rows 23–24 once more, then rep row 23 once more.
Bind (cast) off.*
Carefully unpick A from cast-on edge and slip 10 sts onto needle.
Rep from * to *.

FINISHING
Weave in all loose ends, weaving in ends on ears very neatly.
Turn body inside out, then roll it back right side out over a rolled-up cotton dishtowel, without stretching knitting out of shape, and steam. Leave to cool and remove tea towel. Pleat center of ears and sew to top of head using backstitch and following photograph for position.
Using mattress stitch and matching the stripes, sew seam from tip of nose to base of chest. Insert toy filling from tail end. Using mattress stitch, sew up tail seam.
Embroider as follows:
The face: for each eye, using black tapestry wool and backstitch, embroider an oval with a vertical line either side of the iris area. Fill in the irises with satin stitch in blue and the areas on either side with satin stitch in white; for the nose using black and satin stitch, embroider over the tip of the knitted nose; for the whiskers, using white make fringe loops (as you would for the ends of a scarf) under stitches on each cheek. See also page 124.

Aggie is always doing laundry—as soon as she has got one lot ready and dry, another load is ready to be washed. She does the washing for the whole neighborhood. Sometimes she dreams of getting a new job.

Aggie Bear

pattern

HEAD, BODY, and LEGS

Head

Using US 4 (3.50mm) double-pointed needles, the thumb method, and A, cast on 49 sts.

Arrange the stitches over four needles, make sure the stitches are not twisted and use the fifth needle to knit the first and last cast-on stitches together to join into the round. Place round marker at the start of the round. (12 sts on each needle)

Knit 2 rounds.

Thread a short length of waste yarn through a st loop at the end of the last round. This is the center back.

Round 3: K10, M1R, k2 on first/third needle, k2, M1L, k10 on second/fourth needle. (13 sts on each needle)

Round 4: K11, M1R, k2 on first/third needle, k2, M1L, k11 on second/fourth needle. (14 sts on each needle)

Round 5: K12, M1R, k2 on first/third needle, k2, M1L, k12 on second/fourth needle. (15 sts on each needle)

Round 6: K13, M1R, k2 on first/third needle, k2, M1L, k13 on second/fourth needle. (16 sts on each needle)

Knit 1 round.

Round 8: K14, M1R, k2 on first/third needle, k2, M1L, k14 on second/fourth needle. (17 sts on each needle)

Knit 1 round.

Round 10: K15, M1R, k2 on first/third needle, k2, M1L, k15 on second/fourth needle. (18 sts on each needle)

Knit 10 rounds.

Round 21: K14, k2tog, k2 on first/third needle, k2, skpo, k14 on second/fourth needle. (17 sts on each needle)

Knit 24 rounds.

Round 46: K13, k2tog, k2 on first/third needle, k2, skpo, k13 on second/fourth needle. (16 sts on each needle)

Knit 12 rounds.

Round 59: K12, k2tog, k2 on first/third needle, k2, skpo, k12 on second/fourth needle. (15 sts on each needle)

Knit 3 rounds.

Round 63: K15 and move round marker to this point.

Sweater

Change to US 6 (4mm) double-pointed needles and join in B.

Starting with a knit (RS) round, working in Fair Isle, stranding yarn not in use on the WS, and weaving in yarn as required, work color patt from chart. Read every chart round from right to left twice. Work shaping as follows:

Rounds 64–67: Knit 4 rounds.

Cut A and join in C.

Rounds 68–75: Knit 8 rounds.

Join in D.

Round 76: Knit using D.

Round 77: K1, M1R, k to end on first/third needle, k to last st, M1L, k1 on second/fourth needle. (16 sts on each needle)

Round 78: Knit.

Rounds 79–96: Rep rounds 77–78

Size

Completed creature measures approx. 20 in (50cm) tall

Yarn suggestion

Lightweight yarn (such as Debbie Bliss Baby Cashmerino) 2 x 1³/₄oz (50g) balls in A (pink—340025)

Lightweight yarn (such Sublime Cashmere Merino Silk DK) 1 x 1³/₄oz (50g) ball in B (black—Ebony 0013), 1 ball in C (red—Tease 0052), and 1 ball in D (maroon—Rhubarb 0107)

Needles

Set of five double-pointed US 4 (3.5mm) knitting needles

Set of five double-pointed US 6 (4mm) knitting needles

Extras

Round marker

Waste cotton yarn

Tapestry needle

Washable toy filling

Oddments of black and pink tapestry wool for embroidery

Gauge (Tension)

25 sts and 36 rows to 4in (10cm) over st st using US 4 (3.5mm) needles

Abbreviations

See page 126

nine more times. (25 sts on each needle)

Rounds 97–99: Knit 3 rounds.

Cut B, C, and D and join in A.

Body

Change to US 4 (3.50mm) double-pointed needles and rearrange the sts as follows:

Round 100: K40, put the next 20 sts onto a length of waste yarn, cast on 3 sts, k30, slip the next 20 sts onto a length of waste yarn (last 10 sts were knitted at the beg of this round) cast on 3 sts. (66 sts) (15 sts on first needle, 18 sts on second, 15 sts on third, 18 sts on fourth)

Knit 24 rounds.

First leg

Using only four of the five double-pointed needles, rearrange the sts as follows:

Round 125: K15, put the next 33 sts onto a length of waste yarn, k18, cast on 3 sts. (36 sts)

Arrange sts evenly over three double-pointed needles. (12 sts on each needle)

Knit 54 rounds.

***Round 180:** [K1, k2tog] twelve times. (24 sts in total)

Knit 2 rounds.

Round 183: [K2tog] twelve times. (12 sts in total)

Knit 1 round.

Cut A 4in (10cm) from the last stitch on the needle and thread into a tapestry needle. Pass the tapestry needle through all the stitches on the needles in the order they would have been knitted, use the tip of the needle to pull the yarn at the point just after it has passed through the first stitch to draw the stitches tight to the yarn, then pull the yarn tight as it emerges through the last stitch. Secure the end.*

Second leg

With the First Leg to the right, transfer the first 12 sts from the length of waste yarn onto the first double-pointed needle, transfer the second 12 sts from the length of waste yarn onto the second double-pointed needle, transfer the last 9 sts onto the third

needle, and cast on 3 sts.

Knit 55 rounds.

Work as for First Leg from * to *.

First arm

Using only four of the five double-pointed needles, rearrange the sts as follows:

With the center back to the right, transfer the first 8 sts from the length of waste yarn onto the first double-pointed needle, transfer the second 8 sts from the length of waste yarn onto the second double-pointed needle, transfer the last 4 sts onto the third needle, and cast on 3 sts. (8 sts on first and second needles, 7 sts on third)

Knit 12 rounds.

Round 112: [K1, k2tog] seven times, k2. (16 sts in total)

Knit 2 rounds.

Round 115: [K2tog] eight times, k1. (8 sts in total)

Knit 1 round.

As for First Leg, cut A 4in (10cm) from the needle, thread a tapestry needle and pass this through the rem sts, starting with the first st of the round, and draw tight.

Second arm

With First Arm to the right, work as for First Arm.

EARS (make two)

Using US 4 (3.50mm) double-pointed needles, the thumb method, and A, cast on 16 sts.

Arrange the stitches over three needles, make sure the stitches are not twisted and use the fourth needle to knit the first and last cast-on stitches together to join into the round. Place round marker at the start of the round. (5 sts on each needle)

Knit 32 rounds.

Bind (cast) off.

FINISHING

Press pieces gently following directions on the yarn wrapper.

Weave the loose ends into the WS of the

body. Sew the head seam using mattress stitch. Insert toy filling and sew openings under both arms and between the legs closed using mattress stitch.

Bend the ears pieces around and sew to the head, following photograph for position.

Embroider as follows:

The face: for each eye, using black tapestry wool and backstitch, embroider a half-circle; for the mouth, using pink, embroider a cross. See also page 124.

SWEATER

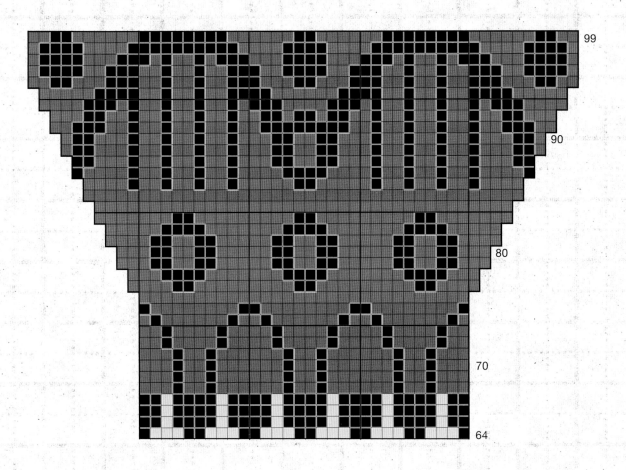

99

90

80

70

64

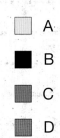 A

B

C

D

Rill, Cyril's first child, is an enthusiastic camper and he loves catching grubs and worms to toast on the camp fire. He's full of energy and is always running around somewhere.

Rill Raccoon~Fox

pattern

Note: two strands of Rowan Scottish Tweed are used together throughout to even out the variable weight of the tweed yarn.

FRONT
First leg
*Using the thumb method and A, cast on 3 sts.
Row 1 (RS): Knit.
Row 2: P1, M1L, p1, M1R, p1. (5 sts)
Row 3: Knit.
Row 4: Purl.
Row 5: Knit.*
Row 6: P4, M1R, p1. (6 sts)
Cut yarn and put sts onto stitch holder.
Second leg
Work as for First Leg from * to *.
Row 6: P1, M1L, p4. (6 sts)
Leave sts on needle and do not cut yarn.
Join legs
Row 7: Knit across 6 sts on needle, cast on 10 sts using the backward loop method, with RS facing knit across 6 sts from stitch holder. (22 sts)
Body
Row 8: P5, p2tog, p8, p2togtbl, p5. (20 sts)
Starting with a k row, work 19 rows st st.
Shape arms
Row 28: P1, M1L, p18, M1R, p1. (22 sts)
Row 29: Cast on 3 sts using the backward loop method, k to end. (25 sts)

Row 30: Cast on 3 sts using the backward loop method, p to end. (28 sts)
Row 31: K1, M1R, k26, M1L, k1. (30 sts)
Starting with a p row, work 2 rows st st.
Row 34: P1, p2tog, p24, p2togtbl, p1. (28 sts)
Row 35: Bind (cast) off 3 sts, k to end. (25 sts)
Row 36: Bind (cast) off 3 sts, p to end. (22 sts)
Row 37: K1, skpo, k16, k2tog, k1. (20 sts)
Head
Join in B.
Using B and starting with a p row, work 6 rows st st.
Cut B and cont in A.
Row 44: Purl.
Shape first ear
Row 45: K8, k2tog, turn.
Work on this set of 9 sts only and put the rem sts on a stitch holder.
Starting with a p row, work 5 rows st st.
Row 51: K6, k2tog, k1. (8 sts)
Starting with a p row, work 11 rows st st.
Row 63: K1, skpo, k2, k2tog, k1. (6 sts)
Starting with a p row, work 3 rows st st.
Row 67: K1, skpo, k2tog, k1. (4 sts)
Row 68: Skpo, k2tog. (2 sts)
Bind (cast) off.
Shape second ear
Put sts on stitch holder onto a needle and

Size
Completed creature measures approx. 8in (20cm) tall
Yarn suggestion
Fine-weight yarn (such as Rowan Scottish Tweed 4 ply) used double 2 x 1oz (25g) balls in A (orange—Sunset 00011) and 1 ball in B (dark brown —Peat 00019)
Needles
Pair of US 4 (3.5mm) knitting needles
Extras
One stitch holder
Tapestry needle
Washable toy filling
Oddments of white and dark brown tapestry wool for embroidery
Gauge (Tension)
18 sts and 34 rows to 4in (10cm) over st st using yarn double and US 4 (3.5mm) needles
Abbreviations
See page 126

with RS facing, rejoin yarn.
Row 45: K2tog, k8. (9 sts)
Starting with a p row, work 5 rows st st.
Row 51: K1, k2tog, k6. (8 sts)
Starting with a p row, work 11 rows st st.
Row 63: K1, skpo, k2, k2tog, k1. (6 sts)
Starting with a p row, work 3 rows st st.
Row 67: K1, skpo, k2tog, k1. (4 sts)
Row 68: Skpo, k2tog. (2 sts)
Bind (cast) off.

BACK

Work as given for Front using A only.

TAIL

Using the thumb method and A, cast on
18 sts.
Row 1: Using A, knit.
Row 2: Using A, purl.
Join in B.
Row 3: Using B, knit.
Row 4: Using B, purl.
Last 4 rows form striped st st patt. Cont in
patt and work shaping as follows:
Work in 24 rows striped st st patt.
Row 29: Using A, [k3, inc] four times, k2.
(22 sts)
Work 15 rows in striped st st patt.
Row 45: Using A, [k4, inc, k4, inc] twice,
k2. (26 sts)
Work 21 rows in striped st st.
Row 67: Using B, [k4, k2tog, k4, k2tog]
twice, k2. (22 sts)
Row 68: Using B, purl.
Row 69: Using A, [k3, k2tog] four times,
k2. (18 sts)
Row 70: Using A, purl.
Cut yarn A.
Row 71: Using B, [k1, k2tog] six times.
(12 sts)
Row 72: [P2tog] six times. (6 sts)
Cut B 4in (10cm) from the last stitch on the
needle and thread into a tapestry needle.
Pass the tapestry needle through all the
stitches on the needles in the order they
would have been knitted, use the tip of the

needle to pull the yarn at the point just after
it has passed through the first stitch to draw
the stitches tight to the yarn, then pull the
yarn tight as it emerges through the last
stitch. Secure the end.

NOSE

Using the thumb method and A, cast on
12 sts.
Row 1 and every alt row (WS): Purl.
Row 2: K10, short-row-wrap the next st,
turn.
Row 4: K8, short-row-wrap the next st, turn.
Row 6: K6, short-row-wrap the next st, turn.
Row 8: K4, short-row-wrap the next st, turn.
Row 10: K2, short-row-wrap the next st,
turn.
Row 12: K2, [pick up the short-row-wrap
and k tog with the wrapped st, k1] five times.
Row 13: Purl.
Rep rows 2–13 once more.
Bind (cast) off.

FINISHING

Press pieces gently following directions on
the yarn wrapper.
Using mattress stitch, sew cast-on and
bound-off edges of nose together. Insert toy
filling into nose. Using mattress stitch, sew
nose to front of head, following photograph
for position.
Using mattress stitch, sew the body pieces
together around the outer edges, weaving
loose ends into seam wherever possible,
and leaving a small opening. Insert toy filling
and sew opening closed.
Using mattress stitch, sew tail pieces
together around the outer edge, leaving the
cast-on edges open. Weave in loose ends,
insert toy filling, and sew cast-on edge to
back body piece, centered just above legs.
Embroider as follows:
The face: for each eye, working on the
brown band and using dark brown tapestry
wool and backstitch, embroider an oval with
a vertical line either side of the iris area. Fill
in the irises with satin stitch in dark brown
and the areas on either side with satin stitch
in white; for the nose, using dark brown and
satin stitch, embroider over the tip of the
knitted nose. See also page 124.

Stick the snail is a funny-looking fellow.
He is very slow but a bit of a perfectionist—
everything he does is done well. He even
polishes his shell twice a day. Stick has the
best shell in town, everyone admires it, which
makes all Stick's hard work worthwhile.

Stick Snail

pattern

BODY and HEAD

Tail

Using the thumb method and A, cast on 37 sts.

Arrange the stitches over three needles, make sure the stitches are not twisted and use the fourth needle to knit the first and last cast-on stitches together to join into the round. Place round marker at the start of the round. (12 sts on each needle)

Knit 63 rounds.

Now work back and forth on the three needles in rows, not rounds.

Row 64: K34, short-row-wrap the next st, turn.

Row 65: Sl1, p31, short-row-wrap the next st, turn.

Row 66: Sl1, k29, short-row-wrap the next st, turn.

Row 67: Sl1, p27, short-row-wrap the next st, turn.

Row 68: Sl1, k25, short-row-wrap the next st, turn.

Row 69: Sl1, p23, short-row-wrap the next st, turn.

Row 70: Sl1, k21, short-row-wrap the next st, turn.

Row 71: Sl1, p19, short-row-wrap the next st, turn.

Row 72: Sl1, k17, short-row-wrap the next st, turn.

Row 73: Sl1, p15, short-row-wrap the next st, turn.

Row 74: Sl1, k13, short-row-wrap the next st, turn.

Row 75: Sl1, p11, short-row-wrap the next st, turn.

Row 76: Sl1, k9, short-row-wrap the next st, turn.

Row 77: Sl1, p7, short-row-wrap the next st, turn.

Row 78: Sl1, k5, short-row-wrap the next st, turn.

Row 79: Sl1, p3, short-row-wrap the next st, turn.

Row 80: Sl1, k3, pick up the short-row-wrap and k tog with the wrapped st, short-row-wrap the next st, turn.

Row 81: Sl1, p4, pick up the short-row-wrap and p tog with the wrapped st, short-row-wrap the next st, turn.

Row 82: Sl1, k5, [pick up the short-row-wrap and k tog with the wrapped st] twice, short-row-wrap the next st, turn.

Row 83: Sl1, p7, [pick up the short-row-wrap and p tog with the wrapped st] twice, short-row-wrap the next st, turn.

Row 84: Sl1, k9, [pick up the short-row-wrap and k tog with the wrapped st] twice, short-row-wrap the next st, turn.

Row 85: Sl1, p11, [pick up the short-row-wrap and p tog with the wrapped st] twice, short-row-wrap the next st, turn.

Row 86: Sl1, k13, [pick up the short-row-wrap and k tog with the wrapped st] twice, short-row-wrap the next st, turn.

Row 87: Sl1, p15, [pick up the short-row-wrap and p tog with the wrapped st] twice, short-row-wrap the next st, turn.

Row 88: Sl1, k17, [pick up the short-row-wrap and k tog with the wrapped st] twice, short-row-wrap the next st, turn.

Row 89: Sl1, p19, [pick up the short-row-wrap and p tog with the wrapped st] twice, short-row-wrap the next st, turn.

Row 90: Sl1, k21, [pick up the short-row-wrap and k tog with the wrapped st] twice, short-row-wrap the next st, turn.

Row 91: Sl1, p23, [pick up the short-row-wrap and p tog with the wrapped st] twice, short-row-wrap the next st, turn.

Row 92: Sl1, k25, [pick up the short-row-wrap and k tog with the wrapped st] twice, short-row-wrap the next st, turn.

Row 93: Sl1, p27, [pick up the short-row-wrap and p tog with the wrapped st] twice, short-row-wrap the next st, turn.

Row 94: Sl1, k29, [pick up the short-row-wrap and k tog with the wrapped st] twice,

Size

Completed creature measures approx.
8¼in (21cm) tall

Yarn suggestion

Lightweight yarn (such as Rowan Wool Cotton) 1 x 1¾oz (50g) ball in A (light brown—Dream 929)

Lightweight yarn (such as Rowan Pure Wool DK): 1 x 1¾oz (50g) ball in B (pink—Petal 024)

Leftover lightweight yarns from your stash

Needles

Set of four double-pointed US 2 (3mm) knitting needles

Extras

Round marker

Waste cotton yarn

Tapestry needle

Washable toy filling

Oddments of black, white, and pink tapestry wool for embroidery

Gauge (Tension)

25 sts and 36 rows to 4in (10cm) over st st using US 2 (3mm) needles

Abbreviations

See page 126

short-row-wrap the next st, turn.

Row 95: Sl1, p31, [pick up the short-row-wrap and p tog with the wrapped st] twice, p1, turn.

Row 96: Sl1, k34, pick up the short-row-wrap and k tog with the wrapped st.
Now work in rounds once more.

Round 97: Pick up the horizontal bar between the last and first sts of the round as if to M1R and k tog this bar with the first st, k to the end of the round.

Rounds 98–139: Knit 42 rounds.

First eye stalk

Round 140: K9, put 18 sts onto a length of waste yarn, cast on 1 st, k9. Rearrange stitches on the double-pointed needles so that there are 6 sts on the first and second needles and 7 sts on the third.
Knit 20 rounds.

Round 161: [K1, k2tog] six times, k1.
(4 sts on the first and second needles, 5 sts on the third)

Round 162: Knit.

Round 163: [K2tog, k1] four times, k1.
(9 sts in total)

Round 164: Knit.
Cut A 4in (10cm) from the last stitch on the needle and thread onto a tapestry needle. Pass the tapestry needle through all the stitches on the needles in the order they would have been knitted, use the tip of the needle to pull the yarn at the point just after it has passed through the first stitch to draw the stitches tight to the yarn, then pull the yarn tight as it emerges through the last stitch. Secure the end.

Second eye stalk

Transfer the next 18 sts from the waste onto two double-pointed needles, rejoin yarn with front facing,

Round 140: To starting working in the round, use a third needle to pick up 1 st from the base of First Eye Stalk, k6, use a fourth needle to k6, Use the needle that has now become free to k6, pick up 1 st from the base of the First Eye Stalk and cast on

1 st. (7 sts on the first needle, 6 sts on the second, 8 sts on the third)
Place round marker at the start of the round.

Round 141: K2tog, k5 on the first needle, k6 on the second needle, k5, k2tog, k1 on the third needle. (6 sts on the first and second needles, 7 sts on the third)

Rounds 142–160: Knit 19 rounds.

Round 161: [K1, k2tog] six times, k1.
(4 sts on the first and second needles, 5 sts on the third)

Round 162: Knit.

Round 163: [K2tog, k1] four times, k1.
(9 sts in total)

Round 164: Knit.
As for First Eye Stalk, cut A 4in (10cm) from the needle, thread a tapestry needle and pass this through the rem sts, starting with the first st of the round, and draw tight.

SHELL

Using the thumb method and B, cast on 37 sts.
Arrange the stitches over three needles, make sure the stitches are not twisted and use the fourth needle to knit the first and last cast-on stitches together to join into the round. Place round marker at the start of the round. (12 sts on each needle)

Rounds 1–2 (WS): Using B, knit.
Join leftover yarn. Leaving any ends to the outside (WS).

Round 3–4: Using leftover yarn, knit.
Rep the last 4 rounds, twisting the yarns at each color change on the outside (WS), until the work measures 39in (100cm).
Bind (cast) off.

FINISHING

Press pieces gently following directions on the yarn wrapper.
Weave in the loose ends in the body, insert toy filling, and sew opening closed using mattress stitch.
Weave in the loose ends in the shell, sew cast-on edge opening closed. Turn inside

out, coil up the tube for about 12in (30cm) without any filling, then insert a little toy filling, and gradually build up the amount of filling while continuing to roll the tube, sewing the coils together as it is rolled. Reduce the amount of toy filling toward the end and sew opening closed. Sew the shell to the body, following the photograph for position.
Embroider as follows:
The face: for each eye, using dark brown tapestry wool and backstitch, embroider an oval with a vertical line either side of the iris area. Fill in the irises with satin stitch in dark brown and the areas on either side with satin stitch in white; for the mouth, using pink and backstitch, embroider a double horizontal line. See also page 124.

Angry Ginger is always grumpy, sometimes he is grumpy for no reason at all. Most of his friends know he is grumpy so they take no notice of him, which makes him even more grumpy! He has a soft spot for gingerbread— that can usually cheer him up.

Angry Ginger

pattern

Note: yarns A, B, and C are worked held together throughout.

HEAD, BODY, and LEGS
Using the thumb method and A, B, and C held together, cast on 6 sts onto one needle.

Round 1 (WS): To start working in the round, slip half the stitches onto a second needle and position the two needles side by side with the first cast-on stitch and the last cast-on stitch adjacent on separate needles. Use a third needle to start knitting the round starting with the first cast-on stitch and working two stitches. Use a fourth needle to knit the next two stitches, one from each of the original two needles. (2 sts on each needle.) Complete knitting the round with the needle that has now become free. Place round marker at the start of the round.

Head
Round 2: [Inc] six times. (4 sts on each needle)
Round 3: Knit.
Round 4: [K1, M1] twelve times. (8 sts on each needle)
Rounds 5–6: Knit.
Round 7: [K3, inc] six times. (10 sts on each needle)
Knit 20 rounds.
Round 28: [K4, inc] six times. (12 sts on each needle)
Knit 2 rounds.

Shape arms
Round 31: K6, double-inc, k2, double-inc, k2 on the first needle, k12 on the second needle, k2, double-inc, k2, double-inc, k6 on the third needle. (16 sts on first needle, 12 sts on second, 16 sts on third)
Round 32: Knit.
Round 33: K16, turn work, p8 across the sts just worked, turn work and k8 on the first needle, k12 on the second needle, k8, turn work, p8 across the sts just worked, turn work and k16 on the third needle.
Round 34: K6, [skpo] twice, k2, [k2tog] twice on the first needle, k12 on the second needle, [skpo] twice, k2, [k2tog] twice, k6 on the third needle. (12 sts on each needle)

Body
Knit 16 rounds.

First leg
Round 51: [K14, bind (cast) off 3 sts] twice. Put the 15 sts not attached to the working yarn onto a length of waste yarn.
*Round 52: To start working in the round, k until 6 sts worked after bind (cast) off, use the free needle to k6, use the free needle to k3, cast on 3 sts using the backward loop method. (6 sts on each needle)
Knit 46 rounds.
Round 99: [K1, skpo, k1, k2tog] three times. (4 sts on each needle)
Knit 2 rounds.
Round 102: [Skpo, k2tog] three times. (2 sts on each needle)
Round 103: Knit.

Size
Completed creature measures approx. 14¹/₂in (36cm) tall

Yarn suggestion
Lightweight yarn (such as Rowan All Seasons Cotton) 1 x 1³/₄oz (50g) ball in A (orange—Tangerine 230)

Superfine-weight yarn (such as Rowan Kidsilk Haze) 1 x 1oz (25g) ball in B (burgundy—Blood 627)

Superfine-weight metallic yarn (such as Twilley's Washable Goldfingering) 1 x 1oz (25g) ball in C (gold—02)

Needles
Set of four double-pointed US 6 (4mm) knitting needles

Extras
Round marker

Waste yarn

Tapestry needle

Washable toy filling

Oddments of dark brown, green, and white tapestry wool for embroidery

Gauge (Tension)
16 sts and 28 rows to 4in (10cm) over st st using US 6 (4mm) needles

Abbreviations
See page 126

Cut yarns 4in (10cm) from the last stitch on the needle and thread into a tapestry needle. Pass the tapestryneedle through all the stitches on the needles in the order in which they would have been knitted, use the tip of the needle to pull the yarn at the point just after it has passed through the first stitch to draw the stitches tight to the yarn, then pull the yarn tight as it emerges through the last stitch. Secure the end.*

Second leg

Transfer the 15 sts from the waste yarn onto two double-pointed needles, rejoin yarn with First Leg to the right on the first st after what will become the gap between the legs. Work as for First Leg from * to *.

FINISHING

Press pieces gently following directions on the yarn wrapper.

Weave in the loose ends on the knit side (WS). Insert toy filling then sew opening between the legs closed using mattress stitch. Work a line of running stitch around each arm bump, draw tight and secure. Embroider as follows:

The face: for each eye, using dark brown tapestry wool and backstitch, embroider an oval with a vertical line either side of the iris area. Fill in the irises with satin stitch in green and the areas on either side with satin stitch in white; for the eyebrows, using dark brown and backstitch, embroider a slanting line above each eye; for the mouth, using dark brown and backstitch, embroider an oval opening and outline the teeth. Fill in the teeth with satin stitch in white.

The chest: using dark brown and straight stitches, embroider short, random lines. See also page 124.

Petra Poodle

Petra is a proud dog, she has excellent
posture, is very conscious of her good
looks, and likes to be perfectly groomed
at all times. She loves a good cup of tea
after a long walk.

pattern

FRONT

Using A and the cable method, cast on 40 sts.

Starting with a k row, work 56 rows st st.

Shape back

Row 57 (RS): K33, put last 7 sts on stitch holder.

Row 58: Purl. (33 sts)

Row 59: K to last 3 sts, k2tog, k1. (32 sts)

Row 60: P1, p2tog, p to end. (31 sts)

Rep rows 59–60 twice more. (27 sts)

Row 65: K to last 3 sts, k2tog, k1. (26 sts)

Row 66: Purl.

Rep rows 65–66 six more times. (20 sts)

Row 79: K to last 3 sts, k2tog, k1. (19 sts)

Row 80: Purl.

Row 81: Knit.

Row 82: Purl.

Rep rows 79–82 twice more. (17 sts)

*Neck

Starting with a k row, work 24 rows st st.

Shape head

Row 115: K1, M1R, k to last st, M1L, k1. (19 sts)

Row 116: Purl.

Rep rows 115–116 six more times. (31 sts)

Starting with a k row, work 4 rows st st.

Row 133: K1, skpo, k to last 3 sts, k2tog, k1. (29 sts)

Row 134: Purl.

Rep rows 133–134 once more. (27 sts)

Row 137: K1, skpo, k to last 3 sts, k2tog, k1. (25 sts)

Row 138: P1, p2tog, p to last 3 sts, p2togtbl, p1. (23 sts)

Rep rows 137–138 twice more. (15 sts)

Row 143: K1, [skpo] twice, k to last 5 sts, [k2tog] twice, k1. (11 sts)

Row 144: P1, [p2tog] twice, p1, [p2togtbl] twice, p1. (7 sts)

Bind (cast) off.*

Shape tail

Put 7 sts on stitch holder onto a needle and with RS facing, rejoin yarn.

Starting with a k row, work 8 rows st st.

Next row: K1, skpo, k1, k2tog, k1. (5 sts)

Next row: Purl.

Bind (cast) off.

BACK

Using A, cast on 40 sts.

Starting with a k row, work 56 rows st st.

Shape back

Row 57 (RS): K7, put these 7 sts on stitch holder, k to end.

Row 58: Purl. (33 sts)

Row 59: K1, skpo, k to end. (32 sts)

Row 60: P to last 3 sts, p2togtbl, p1. (31 sts)

Rep rows 59–60 twice more. (27 sts)

Row 65: K1, skpo, k to end. (26 sts)

Row 66: Purl.

Rep rows 65–66 six more times. (20 sts)

Row 79: K1, skpo, k to end. (19 sts)

Row 80: Purl.

Row 81: Knit.

Row 82: Purl.

Rep rows 79–82 twice more. (17 sts)

Work as for Front from * to *.

Shape tail

Put 7 sts on stitch holder onto a needle and with WS facing, rejoin yarn.

Starting with a p row, work 7 rows st st.

Next row: K1, skpo, k1, k2tog, k1. (5 sts)

Next row: Purl.

Bind (cast) off.

BASE

Using A and the cable method, cast on 3 sts.

Row 1: Knit.

Row 2: Purl.

Row 3: K1, M1R, k to last st, M1L, k1. (5 sts)

Row 4: Purl.

Rep rows 3–4 eight more times. (21 sts)

Starting with a k row, work 22 rows st st.

Row 43: K1, skpo, k to last 3 sts, k2tog, k1. (19 sts)

Size

Completed creature measures approx. 16½in (42cm) tall, including head pompom

Yarn suggestion

Lightweight yarn (such as Debbie Bliss Cashmerino DK) 2 x 1¾oz (50g) balls in A (cream—18002)

Fine-weight yarn (such as Debbie Bliss Rialto 4 ply) 1 x 1¾oz (50g) ball in B (cream—01)

Needles

Pair of US 3 (3.25mm) knitting needles

Other materials

One stitch holder

Tapestry needle

Washable toy filling

(6 x 4 in 15 x 10cm) of thick wool felt or cardboard

Pins

Oddments of black, pale green, and white tapestry wool for embroidery

24 x ½in (60 x 1cm) of green craft felt

Gauge (Tension)

27 sts and 36 rows to 4in (10cm) over st st using US 3 (3.25mm) needles

Abbreviations

See page 126

Row 44: Purl.

Rep rows 43–44 seven more times. (5 sts)

Row 59: Skpo, k1, k2tog. (3 sts)

Row 60: Purl.

Bind (cast) off.

NOSE

Using A and the cable method, cast on 12 sts.

Row 1 (WS) and every alt row: Purl.

Row 2: K8, short-row-wrap the next st, turn.

Row 4: K4, short-row-wrap the next st, turn.

Row 6: K4, [pick up the short-row-wrap and k tog with the wrapped st, k3] twice.

Row 7: Purl.

Rep rows 2–7 four more times.

Bind (cast) off.

EARS (make two)

Using A, cast on 9 sts.

Row 1: K1, p1, k5, p1, k1.

Row 2: K1, p7, k1.

Rep rows 1–2 fifteen more times.

Row 33: K1, p1, skpo, k1, k2tog, p1, k1. (7 sts)

Row 34: K1, p5, k1.

Row 35: K1, p1, s2tog, k1, psso, p1, k1. (5 sts)

Row 36: [K1, p1] twice, k1.

Rep row 36 twice more.

Cut yarn leaving a 8in (20cm) tail. Pass yarn through rem 5 sts and pull up tight.

FINISHING

Weave in loose ends on ears very neatly. Press knitted pieces following instructions on the yarn wrapper.

Using mattress stitch, sew cast-on and bound-off edges of nose together. Insert toy filling into nose. Using chain stitch or mattress stitch as preferred, sew nose to front of head, following photograph for position.

Using mattress stitch, sew body pieces together around the outer edges from cast-on edge, around body and head, and down to other end of cast-on edge, weaving loose ends into the seam wherever possible. Lay base on felt or cardboard and draw around it. Cut out shape, cutting ³/₄in (5mm) inside drawn line. Lay felt or card shape on WS of knitted base piece. Pin knitted base piece into opening in bottom of the body and, using mattress stitch, sew in place, leaving a small opening. Insert toy filling and sew opening closed.

Place ear against side of head, following photograph for position, and place a pin in the head at the top (cast-on edge) of ear. Lay ear right side down across top of head with cast-on edge against pin. Using backstitch, sew across cast-on edge to sew ear to head. Fold ear down over line of sewing.

Using B, make three pompoms approx. 1¹/₄in (3cm) in diameter and one approx. 4in (10cm) in diameter. Sew one small pompom to end of each ear and to top of tail and sew large pompom to top of head. Tie strip of craft felt in a bow around neck.

Embroider as follows:

The face: for each eye, using black tapestry wool and backstitch, embroider an oval with a vertical line either side of the iris area. Fill in the irises with satin stitch in pale green and the areas on either side with satin stitch in white; for the nose, using black and satin stitch, embroider over the tip of the knitted nose. See also page 124.

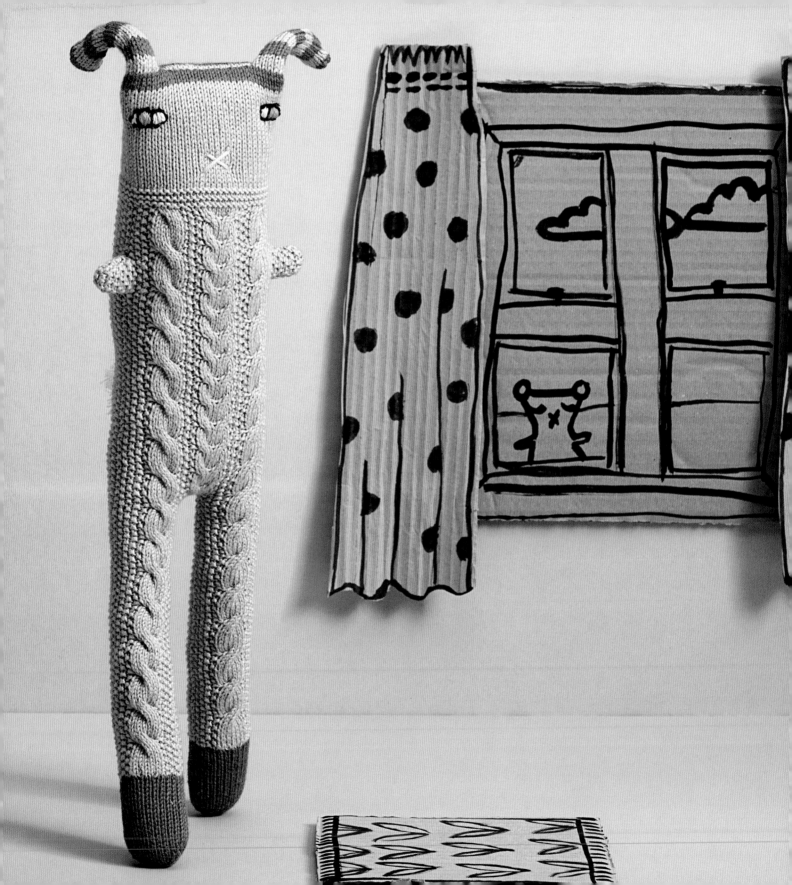

Vanessa is a fitness fanatic—she's been doing gymnastics
since she was young—and fills her days with a strict
regime of yoga, pilates, and jogging.

Vanessa Hare

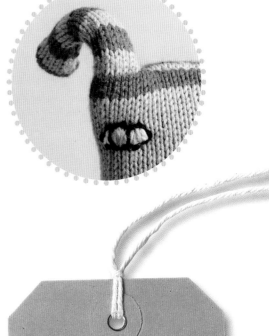

pattern

FRONT
Right leg
Using the cable method and A, cast on 8 sts.

Row 1 (RS): Knit.

Row 2: Purl.

Row 3: K2, M1R, k to last 2 sts, M1L, k2. (10 sts)

Row 4: Purl.

Rep rows 3–4 twice more. (14 sts)

Starting with a k row, work 15 rows st st. Cut A and join in B.

Row 24: Purl.

Row 25: [K1, p1] twice, k2, M1R, k2, M1L, k2, [p1, k1] twice. (16 sts)

Row 26: P2, k1, p1, k1, p6, k1, p1, k1, p2.

Row 27: [K1, p1] twice, k8, [p1, k1] twice.

Rep rows 26–27 three more times, then rep row 26 once more.

Row 35: [K1, p1] twice, k1, C6F, [k1, p1] twice, k1.

Rep rows 26–35 six more times.

Row 96: P2, k1, p1, k1, p6, k1, p1, k1, p2.

Row 97: [K1, p1] twice, k8, [p1, k1] twice.

Rep rows 96–97 twice more, then rep row 96 once more.

Cut yarn and put sts onto stitch holder.

Left leg
Work as for Right Leg, but working C6B instead of C6F.

Leave sts on needle and do not cut yarn.

Join legs
Row 1 (RS): [K1, p1] twice, k8, [p1, k1] twice across sts on needle, cast on 4 sts, [k1, p1] twice, k8, [p1, k1] twice across sts

on stitch holder. (36 sts)

Body
Row 2: P2, k1, p1, k1, p6, k1, p1, k1, p8, k1, p1, k1, p6, k1, p1, k1, p2.

Row 3: [K1, p1] twice, k1, C6B, k1, p1, k10, p1, k1, C6F, [k1, p1] twice, k1.

Row 4: P2, k1, p1, k1, p6, k1, p1, k1, p8, k1, p1, k1, p6, k1, p1, k1, p2.

Row 5: [K1, p1] twice, k8, p1, k10, p1, k8, [p1, k1] twice.

Rep rows 4–5 once more, then rep row 4 once more.

Row 9: [K1, p1] twice, k8, p1, k1, C4B, C4F, k1, p1, k8, [p1, k1] twice.

***Rows 10–11:** As rows 4–5.

Row 12: As row 4.

Row 13: As row 3

Row 14: As row 4.

Row 15: As row 9.

Rows 16–19: As rows 4–5 twice.

Row 20: As row 4.

Row 21: As row 9.

Row 22: As row 4.

Row 23: As row 3

Rows 24–25: As rows 4–5.

Row 26: As row 4.

Row 27: As row 9*.

Rows 28–31: As rows 4–5 twice.

Row 32: As row 4.

Row 33: [K1, p1] twice, k1, C6B, k1, p1, k1, C4B, C4F, k1, p1, k1, C6F, [k1, p1] twice, k1.

Rows 34–37: As rows 4–5 twice.

Row 38: As row 4.

Row 39: As row 9.

Size
Completed creature measures approx. 22in (55cm) tall, including ears

Yarn suggestion
Lightweight yarn (such as Rowan Wool Cotton) 1 x 1³/₄oz (50g) ball in A (mauve—Billberry Fool 959) and 2 balls in B (lilac—Hiss 952)

Fine-weight yarn (such as Rowan Pure Wool 4 ply) small amount in C (cream—Snow 412)

Needles
Pair of US 1 (2.5mm) knitting needles

Extras
Cable needle

One stitch holder

Tapestry needle

Washable toy filling

Oddments of black, blue, white, and pink tapestry wool for embroidery

Gauge (Tension)
28 sts and 49 rows to 4in (10cm) over seed st using US 1 (2.5mm) needles

Abbreviations
See page 126

Rep from * to *.

Rows 58–59: As rows 4–5.

Shape arms

Row 60: Cast on 6 sts, p2, [k1, p1] four times, k1, p6, k1, p1, k1, p8, k1, p1, k1, p6, k1, p1, k1, p2. (42 sts)

Row 61: Cast on 6 sts, [k1, p1] five times, k8, p1, k10, p1, k8, [p1, k1] five times. (48 sts)

Row 62: P2, [k1, p1] four times, k1, p6, k1, p1, k1, p8, k1, p1, k1, p6, [k1, p1] four times, k1, p2.

Row 63: [K1, p1] five times, k1, C6B, k1, p1, k1, C4B, C4F, k1, p1, k1, C6F, [k1, p1] five times, k1.

Row 64: As row 62.

Row 65: [K1, p1] five times, k8, p1, k10, p1, k8, [p1, k1] five times.

Rows 66–67: As rows 64–65.

Row 68: Bind (cast) off 6 sts, [p1, k1] twice, p6, k1, p1, k1, p8, k1, p1, k1, p6, [k1, p1] four times, k1, p2. (42 sts)

Row 69: Bind (cast) off 6 sts, p1, k1, p1, k8, p1, k1, C4B, C4F, k1, p1, k8, [p1, k1] twice. (36 sts)

Rows 70–71: As rows 4–5.

Row 72: As row 4.

Row 73: As row 3.

Row 74: As row 4.

Row 75: As row 9.

Rows 76–79: As rows 4–5 twice.

Row 80: As row 4.

Row 81: As row 9.

Row 82: As row 4.

Row 83: [K1, p1] twice, k1, slip next 3 sts onto cable needle and hold at back, knit next 3 sts on left-hand needle tog with 3 sts on cable needle, k1, p1, k10, p1, k1, slip next 3 sts onto cable needle and hold at front, knit next 3 sts on left-hand needle tog with 3 sts on cable needle, [k1, p1] twice, k1. (30 sts)

Collar

Row 84 (WS): Knit.

Knit 4 more rows.

Head

Starting with a k row, work 24 rows st st.

Join in A.

Work 4 rows st st.

Change to B.

Row 117: Knit.

Shape first ear

Row 118: P8, put these 8 sts onto stitch holder, bind (cast) off until 7 sts rem on left-hand needle, p7.

Cont work on these 8 sts.

**Row 119: Knit.

Row 120: Purl.

Change to A.

Cont work in 4-row stripe patt until 7 more stripes completed.

Bind (cast) off.**

Shape second ear

Put sts on stitch holder onto a needle and with RS facing, rejoin yarn.

Work as for First Ear from ** to **.

BACK

Left leg

*Using the cable method and A, cast on 8 sts.

Row 1 (RS): Knit.

Row 2: Purl.

Row 3: K2, M1R, k2, M1L, k2, M1L, k2. (11 sts)

Row 4: Purl.

Row 5: K2, M1R, k to last 2 sts, M1L, k2. (13 sts)

Row 6: Purl.

Rep rows 5–6 once more. (15 sts)

Starting with a k row, work 15 rows st st.

Cut A and join in B.

Row 24: Purl.

Row 25: [K1, p1] to last st, k1.

Row 26: P2, [k1, p1] to last st, p1.

Rows 25–26 establish seed st with selvedge.

Cont as set until 79 rows of B worked.*

Cut yarn and put sts on stitch holder.

Right leg

Work as for Left Leg from * to *.

Leave sts on needle and do not cut yarn.

Join legs

Row 1 (RS): Seed across sts on needle, cast on 3 sts, seed across sts on holder. (33 sts)

Body

Row 2: P2, [k1, p1] to last st, p1.

Row 3: [K1, p1] to last st, k1.

Rows 2–3 establish seed st with selvedge.

Cont as set until 59 rows of body worked.

Shape arms

Row 60: Cast on 6 sts, p2, [k1, p1] to last st, p1. (39 sts)

Row 61: Cast on 6 sts, [k1, p1] to last st, k1. (45 sts)

Work 6 rows in seed st as set.

Row 68: Bind (cast) off 6 sts, [p1, k1] to last st, p1. (39 sts)

Row 69: Bind (cast) off 6 sts, [p1, k1] to last st. (33 sts)

Row 70: P2, [k1, p1] to last st, p1.

Row 71: [K1, p1] to last st, k1.

Cont in seed st as set until 83 rows of body worked.

Collar

Row 84 (WS): K1, k2tog, k13, k2tog, k12, k2tog, k1. (30 sts).

Knit 4 rows.

Head

Starting with a k row, work 24 rows st st.

Join in A.

Work 4 rows st st.

Change to B.

Row 117: Knit.

Shape first ear

Row 118: P8, put these 8 sts onto stitch holder, bind (cast) off until 7 sts rem on left-hand needle, p7.

Cont work on these 8 sts.

**Row 119: Knit.

Row 120: Purl.

Change to A.

Cont work in 4-row stripe patt until 7 more stripes completed.

Bind (cast) off.**

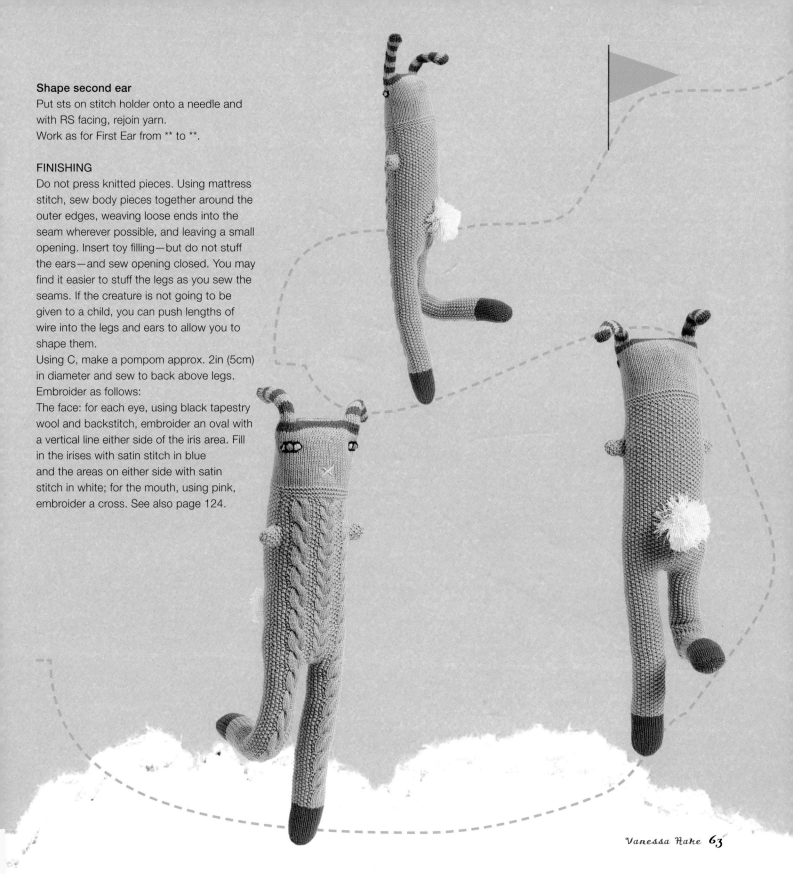

Shape second ear

Put sts on stitch holder onto a needle and with RS facing, rejoin yarn.

Work as for First Ear from ** to **.

FINISHING

Do not press knitted pieces. Using mattress stitch, sew body pieces together around the outer edges, weaving loose ends into the seam wherever possible, and leaving a small opening. Insert toy filling—but do not stuff the ears—and sew opening closed. You may find it easier to stuff the legs as you sew the seams. If the creature is not going to be given to a child, you can push lengths of wire into the legs and ears to allow you to shape them.

Using C, make a pompom approx. 2in (5cm) in diameter and sew to back above legs. Embroider as follows:

The face: for each eye, using black tapestry wool and backstitch, embroider an oval with a vertical line either side of the iris area. Fill in the irises with satin stitch in blue and the areas on either side with satin stitch in white; for the mouth, using pink, embroider a cross. See also page 124.

Like cupcakes, donuts are a perfect treat —delicious and so low-fat! They also make excellent pincushions.

Iced Donut

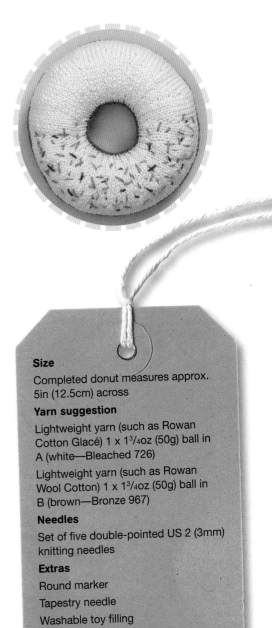

pattern

DONUT

Frosting

Using the thumb method and A, cast on 113 sts.

Arrange the stitches over four needles, make sure the stitches are not twisted and use the fifth needle to knit the first and last cast-on stitches together to join into the round. Place round marker at the start of the round. (28 sts on each needle)

Knit 5 rounds.

Round 6: [K5, k2tog] sixteen times.
(24 sts on each needle)
Knit 2 rounds.

Round 9: [K4, k2tog] sixteen times.
(20 sts on each needle)
Knit 2 rounds.

Round 12: [K3, k2tog] sixteen times.
(16 sts on each needle)
Knit 2 rounds.

Round 15: [K2, k2tog] sixteen times.
(12 sts on each needle)
Knit 2 rounds.

Round 18: [K1, k2tog] sixteen times.
(8 sts on each needle)
Knit 2 rounds.
Cut A and join in B.

Dough

Knit 8 rounds.

Round 29: [K2, M1R] sixteen times.
(12 sts on each needle)
Knit 2 rounds.

Round 32: [K3, M1R] sixteen times.
(16 sts on each needle)
Knit 2 rounds.

Round 35: [K4, M1R] sixteen times.
(20 sts on each needle)
Knit 2 rounds.

Round 38: [K5, M1R] sixteen times.
(24 sts on each needle)
Knit 2 rounds.

Round 41: [K6, M1R] sixteen times.
(28 sts on each needle)
Knit 5 rounds.
Bind (cast) off.

FINISHING

Press piece gently following directions on the yarn wrapper.

Using mattress stitch, sew piece together around the outer edge, weaving loose ends into the seam wherever possible, and leaving a small opening. Insert toy filling and sew opening closed.

Embroider as follows:

The sprinkles: using pink, green, red, and blue tapestry wool and individual straight stitches, embroider random short lines over half the frosting surface.

Size

Completed donut measures approx. 5in (12.5cm) across

Yarn suggestion

Lightweight yarn (such as Rowan Cotton Glacé) 1 x 1³/₄oz (50g) ball in A (white—Bleached 726)

Lightweight yarn (such as Rowan Wool Cotton) 1 x 1³/₄oz (50g) ball in B (brown—Bronze 967)

Needles

Set of five double-pointed US 2 (3mm) knitting needles

Extras

Round marker

Tapestry needle

Washable toy filling

Oddments of pink, green, red, and blue tapestry wool for embroidery

Gauge (Tension)

25 sts and 32 rows to 4in (10cm) over st st using US 2 (3mm) needles

Abbreviations

See page 126

Ralf is the second of Rita and Cyril's offspring and by far the naughtiest. He once locked his brother, Rill, in a cupboard for over an hour!

Bad Ralf

pattern

FRONT

First leg

*Using US 3 (3.25mm) needles, the thumb method, and A, cast on 5 sts.

Row 1 (WS): Purl.

Row 2: K1, M1R, k3, M1L, k1. (7 sts)

Row 3: Purl.

Row 4: Knit.

Row 5: Purl.

Row 6: K1, M1R, k5, M1L, k1. (9 sts)

Row 7: Purl.*

Cut yarn and put sts onto a stitch holder.

Second leg

Work as for First Leg from * to *.

Leave sts on needle and do not cut yarn.

Join legs

Row 8: Knit across 9 sts on needle, cast on 10 sts using the backward loop method, with RS facing knit across 9 sts from stitch holder. (28 sts)

Body

Row 9: P8, p2tog, p8, p2togtbl, p8. (26 sts)

Starting with a k row, work 2 rows st st.

Row 12: K1, skpo, k20, k2tog, k1. (24 sts)

Starting with a p row, work 5 rows st st.

Row 18: K1, skpo, k18, k2tog, k1. (22 sts)

Starting with a p row, work 4 rows st st.

Shape arms

Row 23: P1, M1L, p20, M1R, p1. (24 sts)

Row 24: Cast on 3 sts using the backward loop method, k to end. (27 sts)

Row 25: Cast on 3 sts using the backward loop method, p to end. (30 sts)

Row 26: K1, M1R, k28, M1L, k1. (32 sts)

Starting with a p row, work 2 rows st st.

Row 29: P1, p2tog, p26, p2togtbl, p1. (30 sts)

Row 30: Bind (cast) off 3 sts, k to end. (27 sts)

Row 31: Bind (cast) off 3 sts, p to end. (24 sts)

Row 32: K1, skpo, k18, k2tog, k1. (22 sts)

Starting with a p row, work 3 rows st st.

Head

Join in B.

Using B and starting with a k row, work 4 rows in st st.

Cut B and cont in A.

Starting with a k row, work 2 rows st st.

Shape first ear

Row 42: K1, M1R, k10, turn.

Work on this set of 12 sts only and put the rem sts on a stitch holder.

Row 43: Purl.

Row 44: K1, M1R, k8, k2tog, k1. (12 sts)

Starting with a p row, work 3 rows st st.

Rep rows 44–47 once more.

Row 52: K1, M1R, k8, k2tog, k1. (12 sts)

Row 53: Purl.

Row 54: K1, skpo, k6, k2tog, k1. (10 sts)

Row 55: Purl.

Row 56: K1, skpo, k4, k2tog, k1. (8 sts)

Row 57: Purl.

Row 58: K1, skpo, k2, k2tog, k1. (6 sts)

Row 59: Purl.

Bind (cast) off.

Shape second ear

Put sts on stitch holder onto a needle and with RS facing, rejoin yarn.

Row 42: K10, M1L, k1. (12 sts)

Size

Completed creature measures approx. 6in (16cm) tall

Yarn suggestion

Lightweight yarn (such as Rowan Wool Cotton) 1 x 1¾oz (50g) ball in A (dark brown—Coffee Rich 956) and 1 ball in B (orange—Pumpkin 962)

Needles

Pair of US 3 (3.25mm) knitting needles

Set of four double-pointed US 3 (3.25mm) knitting needles

Extras

One stitch holder

Tapestry needle

Washable toy filling

Oddments of dark brown, blue, and white tapestry wool for embroidery

Gauge (Tension)

23 sts and 35 rows to 4in (10cm) over st st using US 3 (3.25mm) needles

Abbreviations

See page 126

Row 43: Purl.
Row 44: K1, skpo, k8, M1L, k1. (12 sts)
Starting with a p row, work 3 rows st st.
Rep rows 44–47 once more.
Row 52: K1, skpo, k8, M1L, k1. (12 sts)
Row 53: Purl.
Row 54: K1, skpo, k6, k2tog, k1. (10 sts)
Row 55: Purl.
Row 56: K1, skpo, k4, k2tog, k1. (8 sts)
Row 57: Purl.
Row 58: K1, skpo, k2, k2tog, k1. (6 sts)
Row 59: Purl.
Bind (cast) off.

BACK

Work as given for Front using A only.

TAIL

Using US 3 (3.25mm) double-pointed needles,
the thumb method, and A, cast on 25 sts.
Arrange the stitches over three needles,
make sure the stitches are not twisted and
use the fourth needle to knit the first and last
cast-on stitches together to join into the
round. Place round marker at the start of the
round. (8 sts on each needle)
Round 1: [K1, p1] rep to end of round.
Rep round 1 seven more times.
Round 9: [K1, M1R] rep to end of round.
(48 sts)
Join in B.
Round 10: [K1A, k1B] rep to end of round.
Rep round 10 twenty nine more times.
Round 40: [K2togB, skpoA] rep to end of
round. (24 sts)
Round 41: [K1B, k1A] rep to end of round.
Round 42: Rep round 41.
Round 43: [K2togA, skpoB] rep to end of
round. (12 sts)
Round 44: [K1A, k1B] rep to end of round.
Round 45: [K2togB, skpoA] rep to end of
round. (6 sts)
Cut A and B 4in (10cm) from the last stitch
on the needle and thread A into a tapestry
needle. Pass the tapestry needle through all
the stitches on the needles in the order they

would have been knitted, use the tip of the
needle to pull the yarn at the point just after
it has passed through the first stitch to draw
the stitches tight to the yarn, then pull the
yarn tight as it emerges through the last
stitch. Secure the end.

NOSE

Using US 3 (3.25mm) needles, the thumb
method, and A, cast on 16 sts.
Row 1 and every alt row (WS): Purl.
Row 2: K14, short-row-wrap the next
st, turn.
Row 4: K12, short-row-wrap the next
st, turn.
Row 6: K10, short-row-wrap the next
st, turn.
Row 8: K8, short-row-wrap the next st, turn.
Row 10: K6, short-row-wrap the next st, turn.
Row 12: K4, short-row-wrap the next
st, turn.
Row 14: K2, short-row-wrap the next
st, turn.
Row 16: K2, [pick up the short-row-wrap
and knit tog with the wrapped st, k1]
seven times.
Row 17: Purl.
Rep rows 2–17 once more.
Bind (cast) off.

FINISHING

Press pieces gently following directions on
the yarn wrapper.
Using mattress stitch, sew cast-on and
bound-off edges of nose together. Insert toy
filling into nose. Using mattress stitch, sew
nose to front of head, following photograph
for position.
Using mattress stitch, sew the body pieces
together around the outer edges, weaving
loose ends into seam wherever possible,
and leaving a small opening. Insert toy filling
and sew opening closed.
Weave in loose ends on tail, insert toy filling,
and sew opening closed. Sew the tail to the
back, centered just above the legs.
Embroider as follows:
The face: for each eye, working on the
orange band and using dark brown tapestry
wool and backstitch, embroider an oval with
a vertical line either side of the iris area. Fill
in the irises with satin stitch in blue and the
areas on either side with satin stitch in white;
for the nose, using dark brown and satin
stitch, embroider over the tip of the knitted
nose. See also page 124.

Mitten Kitten is very partial to midnight feasts. When everything is quiet she creeps downstairs and fixes herself a treat. So far no one has found out and Mitten would like to keep it that way!

Mitten Kitten

pattern

FRONT

Back leg

Using the thumb method and A, cast on
5 sts.

Row 1 (WS): Purl.

Row 2: K1, M1R, k3, M1L, k1. (7 sts)

Row 3: Purl.

Row 4: Knit.

Row 5: Purl.

Row 6: K1, M1R, k5, M1L, k1. (9 sts)

Starting with a p row, work 2 rows st st.

Row 9: P1, p2tog, p to end. (8 sts)

Cut yarn and put sts onto stitch holder.

Second leg

Using the thumb method and A, cast on
5 sts.

Row 1 (WS): Purl.

Row 2: K1, M1R, k3, M1L, k1. (7 sts)

Starting with a p row, work 3 rows st st.

Row 6: K1, M1R, k5, M1L, k1. (9 sts)

Starting with a p row, work 3 rows st st.

Cut yarn and put sts onto stitch holder.

Third and Fourth legs

Work as for Second Leg.

Leave sts of Fourth leg on needle and do
not cut yarn

Join legs

Row 10: Knit across 9 sts on needle, [cast
on 3 sts using the backward loop method,
with RS facing, knit across 9 sts of the next
leg] twice, cast on 3 sts using the backward
loop method, k5, k2tog, knit across 8 sts of
back leg. (43 sts)

Body

Row 11: P1, p2tog, p4, p2tog, p1,
[p2togtbl, p7, p2tog] twice, p1, p2togtbl,
p8. (36 sts)

Starting with a knit (RS) row, working in
Fair Isle, stranding the yarn not in use on
the WS and weaving in yarn as required,
work color patt from the chart. Work
shaping as follows:

Rows 12–13:

Join in B.

Rows 14–15: Work in st st.

Row 16: K to last 3 sts, k2tog, k1. (35 sts)

Row 17: Purl.

Rows 18–19: Rep rows 16–17 once. (34 sts)

Row 20: K to last 3 sts, k2tog, k1. (33 sts)

Row 21: P1, p2tog, p to end. (32 sts)

Rows 22–23: Rep rows 20–21 once. (30 sts)

Row 24–31: Rep rows 16–17 four times.
(26 sts)

Head

Join in C.

Rows 32–75: Starting with a k row, work
44 rows st st.

Shape first ear

Row 76: K10, put the last 10 sts onto a
stitch holder, bind (cast) off 6 sts, k9.
Work on these 10 sts only for the first ear.

Row 77: P to last 3 sts, p2togtbl, p1. (9 sts)

Row 78: K1, skpo, k to end. (8 sts)

Rows 79–80: Rep rows 77–78 once. (6 sts)

Row 81: Purl.

Row 82: K1, skpo, k to end. (5 sts)

Rows 83–84: Rep rows 81–82 once. (4 sts)

Rows 85–87: Starting with a p row, work
3 rows st st.

Bind (cast) off.

Shape second ear

Put sts on stitch holder onto a needle and with WS facing, rejoin B and C.

Row 77: P1, p2tog, p to end. (9 sts)

Row 78: K to last 3 sts, k2tog, k1. (8 sts)

Rows 79–80: Rep rows 77–78 once. (6 sts)

Row 81: Purl.

Row 82: K to last 3 sts, k2tog, k1.(5 sts)

Rows 83–84: Rep rows 81–82 once. (4 sts)

Rows 85–87: Starting with a p row, work 3 rows st st.

Bind (cast) off.

BACK

Work chart given for Back with written shaping as given for Front, reversing RS of work (to make a pair of pieces) by reading knit for purl and vice versa. See page 118 for reverse shaping tips.

TAIL

Using the thumb method and A, cast on 11 sts.

Starting with a knit (RS) row, working in Fair Isle, stranding the yarn not in use on the WS and weaving in yarn as required, work color patt from the chart.

Rows 1–82: Work in st st.

Bind (cast) off.

FINISHING

Press pieces gently following directions on the yarn wrapper.

Using mattress stitch and C, sew the long edges of the tail together 2 sts in from the edge, leaving the cast-on end open. This technique will fill the tail as you seam it. Following the photograph for position, pin tail to front body. Using mattress stitch, sew body pieces together around the outer edges, catching tail into seam, weaving loose ends into seam wherever possible, and leaving a small opening. Insert toy filling and sew opening closed. If the creature is not going to be given to a child, you can push a length of wire into the tail to allow you to shape it.

Embroider as follows:

The face: for each eye, using black tapestry wool and backstitch, embroider an oval with a wide black line down the center. Fill in the areas on either side with satin stitch in green for the nose and mouth, using pink and backstitch, embroider an inverted triangle with a vertical line descending from the apex. Embroider gently curving lines out to each side; for the whiskers, using black make fringe loops (as you would for the ends of a scarf) under stitches on each cheek. See also page 124.

FRONT

BACK

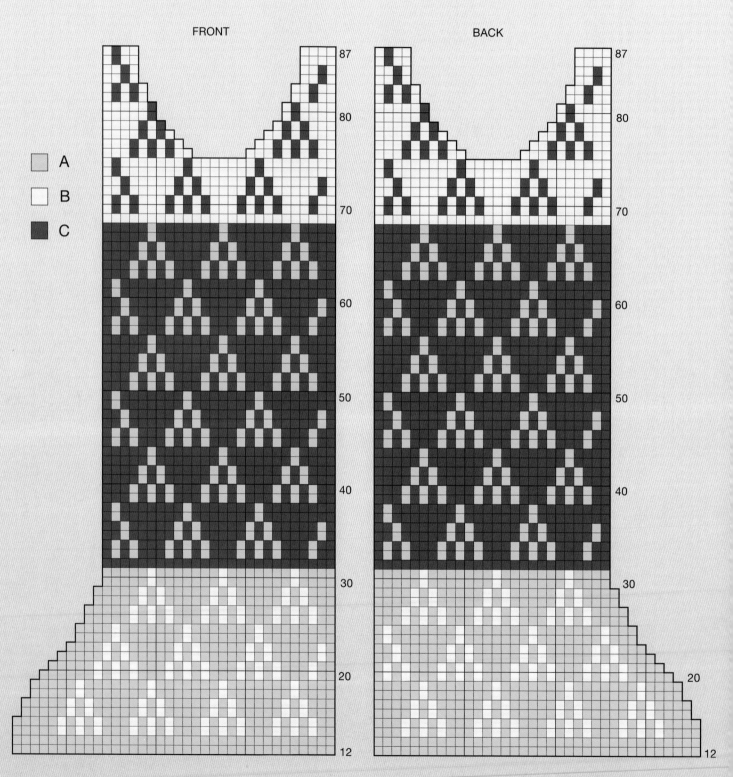

A

B

C

87

80

70

60

50

40

30

20

12

87

80

70

60

50

40

30

20

12

TAIL

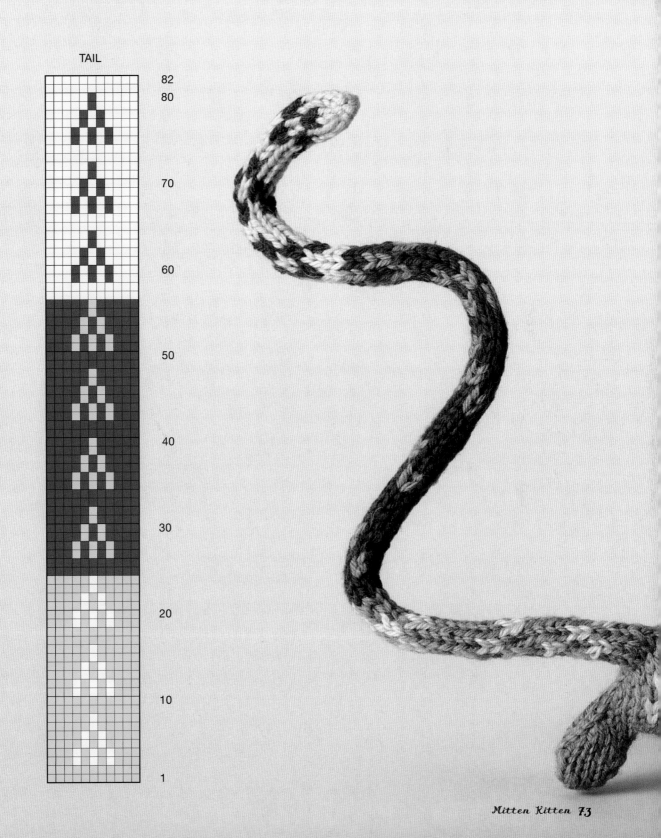

82
80

70

60

50

40

30

20

10

1

Size

Completed creature measures approx.
3^1/$_2$in (9cm) long

Yarn suggestion

Superfine-weight yarn (such as Rowan
Kidsilk Haze) 1 x 10z (25g) ball in
A (dark brown—Villian 584) and 1 ball in
C (cream—Cream 634)

Embroidery floss (thread) (such as DMC embroidery cotton) 1 x skein in B (yellow—728)

Needles

Set of four double-pointed US 0 (2mm)
knitting needles

Pair of US 6 (4mm) knitting needles

Extras

Round marker

Tapestry needle

Washable toy filling

Oddments of black, blue, white, and pink
tapestry wool for embroidery

Gauge (Tension)

30 sts and 36 rows to 4in (10cm) over st st
using A and US 0 (2mm) needles

20 sts and 28 rows to 4in (10cm) over st st
using C and US 6 (4mm) needles

Abbreviations

See page 126

Evel is a busy bee, most of the time he zooms around at 100 miles-an-hour looking for jobs to do. In his spare time he likes doing dangerous aerobatics: loop-the-loop is a favorite.

Evel Bee

pattern

HEAD and BODY

Using US 0 (2mm) double-pointed needles, the thumb method, and A, cast on 6 sts onto one needle.

Round 1 (RS): To start working in the round, slip half the stitches onto a second needle and position the two needles side by side with the first cast-on stitch and the last cast-on stitch adjacent on separate needles. Use a third needle to start knitting the round starting with the first cast-on stitch and working two stitches. Use a fourth needle to knit the next two stitches, one from each of the original two needles. (2 sts on each needle.) Complete knitting the round with the needle that has now become free. Place round marker at the start of the round.

Round 2 (RS): [Inc] six times.
(4 sts on each needle)
Knit 2 rounds.

Round 5: [Inc] twelve times.
(8 sts on each needle)
Knit 2 rounds.

Round 8: [K1, inc] twelve times.
(12 sts on each needle)
Knit 10 rounds.
Join in B.

Rounds 19–20: Using B, knit. (2 rounds)

Rounds 21–23: Using A, knit. (3 rounds)
Rep rounds 19–23 four more times.
Cut B.
Using A, knit 2 rounds.

Round 46: [K1, k2tog] twelve times.
(8 sts on each needle)
Knit 2 rounds.
Insert toy filling.

Round 49: [K2tog] twelve times.
(4 sts on each needle)
Knit 1 round.

Round 51: [K2tog] six times.
(2 sts on each needle)
Cut A 4in (10cm) from the last stitch on the needle and thread into a tapestry needle. Pass the tapestry needle through all the stitches on the knitting needles in the order in which they would have been knitted, use the tip of the needle to pull the yarn at the point just after it has passed through the first stitch to draw the stitches tight to the yarn, then pull the yarn tight as it emerges through the last stitch. Secure the end.

WINGS (both together)

Using US 6 (4mm) needles, the thumb method, and C, cast on 20 sts.

Row 1 (WS): Purl.

Row 2: Knit.

Row 3: P1, M1L, p to last st, M1R, p1.
(22 sts)

Row 4: K1, M1R, k to last st, M1L, k1.
(24 sts)

Row 5: P1, M1L, p to last st, M1R, p1.
(26 sts)
Rep rows 4–5 once more. (30 sts)

Row 8: Knit.

Row 9: Purl.

Row 10: Knit.

Row 11: P1, p2tog, p to last 3 sts, p2togtbl, p1. (28 sts)

Row 12: K1, skpo, k to last 3 sts, k2tog, k1. (26 sts)

Row 13: P1, p2tog, p to last 3 sts, p2togtbl, p1. (24 sts)

Rows 14–15: Rep rows 12–13. (20 sts)

Row 16: Knit.

Row 17: Purl.
Bind (cast) off.

FINISHING

Lightly steam the pieces following directions on the yarn wrapper.
Pleat the center of the wings and backstitch them to the top of the body, following photograph for position.
Embroider as follows:
The face: for each eye, using blue tapestry wool and satin stitch, embroider a stripe for the iris. On either side, embroider stripes with satin stitch in white; for the mouth, using pink and backstitch, embroider a gently curving line. See also page 124.

Bert is a friendly bear. He loves bubble gum and can blow bubbles bigger than his head. He is known for his big appetite and keen sense of smell.

Bert Bear

pattern

FRONT and BACK (both alike)
First leg
*Cast on 8 sts.
Row 1 (RS): Knit.
Row 2: Purl.
Row 3: K2, M1R, k to last 2 sts, M1L, k2. (10 sts)
Row 4: Purl.
Rep rows 3–4 twice more. (14 sts)
Starting with a k row, work 12 rows st st.*
Cut yarn and put sts onto stitch holder.
Second leg
Work as for First Leg from * to *.
Leave sts on needle and do not cut yarn.
Join legs
Knit across 14 sts on needle, cast on 10 sts using the cable method, knit across 14 sts from stitch holder. (38 sts)
Shape body
Starting with a purl row, work 39 rows st st,
Shape arms
Next row: K2, M1R, k to last 2 sts, M1L, k2. (40 sts)
Next row: Purl.
Rep last 2 rows once more. (42 sts)
Next row: Cast on 8 sts, k to end. (50 sts)
Next row: Cast on 8 sts, p to end. (58 sts)
Next row: K2, M1R, k to last 2 sts, M1L, k2. (60 sts)
Next row: Purl.

Rep last 2 rows once more. (62 sts)
Next row: K2, skpo, k to last 4 sts, k2tog, k2. (60 sts)
Next row: Purl.
Rep last 2 rows once more. (58 sts)
Next row: Bind (cast) off 6 sts, k to end. (52 sts)
Next row: Bind (cast) off 6 sts, p to end. (46 sts)
Next row: Bind (cast) off 4 sts, k to end. (42 sts)
Next row: Bind (cast) off 4 sts, p to end. (38 sts)
Starting with a knit row, work 8 rows st st,
Shape head
Next row: K2, M1R, k to last 2 sts, M1L, k2. (40 sts)
Next row: Purl.
Rep last 2 rows twelve more times. (64 sts)
Starting with a knit row, work 6 rows st st.
Shape first ear
Next row: K28, put these 28 sts onto stitch holder, bind (cast) off 8 sts, k to end. Cont work on these 28 sts.
Starting with a purl row, work 3 rows st st.
Next row: K2, skpo, k to end. (27 sts)
Next row: P to last 4 sts, p2togtbl, p2. (26 sts)
Rep last 2 rows once more. (24 sts)
**Starting with a knit row, work 6 rows st st.

Size
Completed creature measures approx. 15½in (38cm) tall

Yarn suggestion
Medium-weight yarn (such as Lion Brand Fishermen's Wool) 1 x 8oz (227g) ball in brown— Nature's Brown 126

Note: *1 ball of Fishermen's Wool will make three bears.*

Needles
Pair of US 3 (3.25mm) knitting needles

Extras
One stitch holder
Tapestry needle
Washable toy filling
Oddments of black, blue, and white tapestry wool for embroidery

Gauge (Tension)
27 sts and 35 rows to 4in (10cm) over st st using US 3 (3.25mm) needles

Abbreviations
See page 126

Next row: K2, skpo, k to last 4 sts, k2tog, k2. (22 sts)

Starting with a purl row, work 3 rows st st. Rep last 4 rows once more. (20 sts)

Next row: K2, skpo, k to last 4 sts, k2tog, k2. (18 sts)

Next row: P2, p2tog, p to last 4 sts, p2togtbl, p2. (16 sts)

Rep last 2 rows twice more. (8 sts)

Next row: K2, skpo, k to last 4 sts, k2tog, k2. (6 sts)

Bind (cast) off purlwise.**

Shape second ear

Put sts on stitch holder onto needle and with WS facing, rejoin yarn to right-hand side of sts.

Starting with a purl row, work 3 rows st st.

Next row: K to last 4 sts, k2tog, k2. (27 sts)

Next row: P2, p2tog, p to end. (26 sts)

Rep last 2 rows once more. (24 sts)

Rep from ** to **.

NOSE

Cast on 4 sts.

Row 1 (RS): Purl.

Row 2: Inc, k to last 2 sts, inc, k1. (6 sts)

Row 3: Inc, p to last 2 sts, inc, p1. (8 sts)

Rep last 2 rows once more, then rep row 2 once more. (14 sts)

Row 7: Purl.

Row 8: As row 2. (16 sts)

Starting with a p row, work 5 rows st st.

Row 14: Skpo, k to last 2 sts, k2tog. (14 sts)

Row 15: Purl.

Row 16: As row 14. (12 sts)

Row 17: P2tog, p to last 2 sts, p2togtbl. (10 sts)

Row 18: As row 14. (8 sts)

Row 19: As row 17. (6 sts)

Row 20: As row 14. (4 sts)

Bind (cast) off.

FINISHING

Block and press knitted pieces, pinning nose into a smooth circular shape and following instructions on the yarn wrapper.

Pin nose to center of face, following photograph for position. Thread a tapestry needle with yarn and using chain stitch, sew around edge of nose to attach it to face. Before completing sewing, insert toy filling into nose. Using mattress stitch, sew body pieces together around the outer edges, weaving loose ends into the seam wherever possible, and leaving a small opening. Insert toy filling and sew opening closed.

Embroider as follows:

The face: for each eye, using black tapestry wool and backstitch, embroider an oval with a vertical line either side of the iris area. Fill in the irises with satin stitch in blue and the areas on either side with satin stitch in white; for the nose and mouth, using black and satin stitch, embroider an inverted triangle with a backstitch vertical line descending from the apex to touch the top of a backstitch circle. Outline one upper tooth in the circle with backstitch and black.

See also page 124.

Fifi Flamingo

Fifi is a big gossip. She always wants to know what's going on and who has done what and she can chat for hours. Once she chatted on the phone to a friend in Australia for seven hours non-stop! The bill was enormous!

Size
Completed creature measures approx. 38in (98cm) from beak to tail

Yarn suggestion
Lightweight yarn (such as Debbie Bliss Prima) 1 x 1³/₄oz (50g) ball in A (black—35701)

Lightweight yarn (such as Debbie Bliss Baby Cashmerino) 1 x 1³/₄oz (50g) ball in B (bright pink—3400129); 1 ball in C (pink—340016)

Needles
Set of four double-pointed US 2 (3mm) knitting needles

Extras
Round marker

Tapestry needle

Washable toy filling

Oddments of black, blue, and white tapestry wool for embroidery

Gauge (Tension)
25 sts and 40 rows to 4in (10cm) over st st using US 2 (3mm) needles

Abbreviations
See page 126

pattern

HEAD and BODY

Beak

Using the thumb method and A, cast on 6 sts onto one needle.

Round 1 (RS): To start working in the round, slip half the stitches onto a second needle and position the two needles side by side with the first cast-on stitch and the last cast-on stitch adjacent on separate needles. Use a third needle to start knitting the round starting with the first cast-on stitch and working two stitches. Use a fourth needle to knit the next two stitches, one from each of the original two needles. (2 sts on each needle.) Complete knitting the round with the needle that has now become free. Place round marker at the start of the round.

Round 2: Knit.

Round 3: [Inc] six times.
(4 sts on each needle)
Knit 2 rounds.

Round 6: [Inc] twelve times.
(8 sts on each needle)
Knit 4 rounds.

Round 11: [K2, M1R] four times on first needle, [K2, M1R] four times on second needle, k8 on third needle. (12 sts on first and second needles, 8 sts on third needle)
Knit 4 rounds.

Round 16: [K3, M1R] four times on first needle, [K3, M1R] four times on second needle, k8 on third needle. (16 sts on first and second needles, 8 sts on third needle)
Knit 36 rounds
Cut A and join in B.

Round 53: Knit.

Round 54: [K1, p1] rep to end of round.
Rep round 54 ten more times.
Cut B and join in C.
Insert toy filling into beak.

Head

Round 65: Knit.

Purl 2 rounds.
Knit 30 rounds

Round 98: [K2, k2tog] ten times.
(12 sts on first and second needles, 6 sts on third needle)
Insert toy filling into head.

Neck

Knit 194 rounds.
Insert toy filling into neck after approx. every 30 rounds knitted.

Body

Round 293: [K3, M1R] ten times.
(16 sts on first and second needles, 8 sts on third needle)
Knit 2 rounds.

Round 296: [K4, M1R] ten times.
(20 sts on first and second needles, 10 sts on third needle)
Knit 2 rounds.

Round 299: [K5, M1R] ten times.
(24 sts on first and second needles, 12 sts on third needle)
Knit 2 rounds.

Round 302: [K6, M1R] ten times.
(28 sts on first and second needles, 14 sts on third needle)
Knit 2 rounds.

Round 305: [K7, M1R] ten times.
(32 sts on first and second needles, 16 sts on third needle)
Knit 30 rounds.
Insert toy filling into body.

Round 336: [K6, k2tog] ten times.
(28 sts on first and second needles, 14 sts on third needle)
Knit 2 rounds.

Round 339: [K5, k2tog] ten times.
(24 sts on first and second needles, 12 sts on third needle)
Knit 4 rounds.

Round 344: [K4, k2tog] ten times.
(20 sts on first and second needles, 10 sts

on third needle)

Knit 8 rounds.

Round 353: [K3, k2tog] ten times.
(16 sts on first and second needles, 8 sts on third needle)

Knit 8 rounds.

Round 362: [K2, k2tog] ten times.
(12 sts on first and second needles, 6 sts on third needle)

Knit 8 rounds.

Insert toy filling.

Round 371: [K1, k2tog] ten times.
(8 sts on first and second needles, 4 sts on third needle)

Knit 8 rounds.

Insert toy filling into body.

Round 380: [K2tog] ten times.
(4 sts on first and second needles, 2 sts on third needle)

Knit 8 rounds.

Round 389: [K2tog] five times.
(2 sts on first and second needles, 1 st on third needle)

Round 390: Knit.

Cut C 4in (10cm) from the last stitch on the needle and thread into a tapestry needle. Pass the tapestry needle through all the stitches on the needles in the order they would have been knitted, use the tip of the needle to pull the yarn at the point just after it has passed through the first stitch to draw the stitches tight to the yarn, then pull the yarn tight as it emerges through the last stitch. Secure the end.

LEGS (make two)

Using the thumb method and B, cast on 12 sts onto one needle. Arrange sts over three needles so that there are 4 sts on each needle.

Place round marker at the start of the round. Knit rounds until the work measures 25in (62cm) from the cast-on edge.

Next round: [K2tog] six times.
(2 sts on each needle)

Next round: Knit.

As for body, cut B 4in (10cm) from the needle, thread a tapestry needle and pass this through the rem sts, starting with the first st of the round, and draw tight.

FINISHING

Press pieces gently following directions on the yarn wrapper.

Note that the legs are not stuffed.

Using mattress stitch, sew the legs to the underside of the body. If the creature is not being given to a child, you can insert a length of wire into the neck and bend it into shape.

Embroider as follows:

The face: for each eye, using black tapestry wool and backstitch, embroider an oval with a vertical line either side of the iris area. Fill in the irises with satin stitch in blue and the areas on either side with satin stitch in white. See also page 124.

Albert comes from a very small place so he doesn't like being around a lot of people and prefers country walks by himself. When he visits the city he has to wear earplugs as he thinks it's all too loud.

Lovely Albert

pattern

HEAD, BODY, and LEGS

Head

Using US 5 (3.75mm) double-pointed needles, the thumb method, and A, cast on 57 sts.

Arrange sts over four needles and use the fifth needle to knit the first and last cast-on sts together to join into the round. Place round marker at start. (14 sts on each needle)
Knit 2 rounds.

Thread a length of waste yarn through st loop at end of last round. This is center back.

Round 3: K13, M1R, k1 on first/third needle, k1, M1L, k13 on second/fourth needle. (15 sts on each needle)

Round 4: K13, M1R, k2 on first/third needle, k2, M1L, k13 on second/fourth needle. (16 sts on each needle)

Round 5: K13, M1R, k3 on first/third needle, k3, M1L, k13 on second/fourth needle. (17 sts on each needle)
Knit 1 round.

Round 7: K13, M1R, k4 on first/third needle, k4, M1L, k13 on second/fourth needle. (18 sts on each needle)
Knit 1 round.

Round 9: K13, M1R, k5 on first/third needle, k5, M1L, k13 on second/fourth needle. (19 sts on each needle)
Knit 1 round.

Round 11: K13, M1R, k6 on first/third needle, k6, M1L, k13 on second/fourth needle. (20 sts on each needle)
Knit 1 round.

Round 13: K13, M1R, k7 on first/third needle, k7, M1L, k13 on second/fourth needle. (21 sts on each needle)
Knit 2 rounds.

Round 16: K13, M1R, k8 on first/third needle, k8, M1L, k13 on second/fourth needle. (22 sts on each needle)
Knit 2 rounds.

Round 19: K13, M1R, k9 on first/third needle, k9, M1L, k13 on second/fourth needle. (23 sts on each needle)
Knit 2 rounds.

Round 22: K13, M1R, k10 on first/third needle, k10, M1L, k13 on second/fourth needle. (24 sts on each needle)

Separate stitches for ears

Round 23: K13, put the next 22 sts onto a length of waste yarn, cast on 4 sts, k26, slip the next 22 sts onto a length of waste yarn, cast on 4 sts, k13. (60 sts)
Arrange 15 stitches on each of four needles.

Body

Knit 7 rounds.

Round 31: K11, k2tog, k2 on first/third needle, k2, skpo, k11 on second/fourth needle. (14 sts on each needle)

Size
Completed creature measures approx. 6^1/$_4$in (16cm) tall

Yarn suggestion
Lightweight yarn (such as Sublime Angora Merino) 1 x 1^3/$_4$oz (50g) ball in A (blue—Dusky 0047) and 1 ball in B (white—Feather 040)

Needles
Set of five double-pointed US 5 (3.75mm) knitting needles
Pair of US 5 (3.75mm) knitting needles.

Extras
Round marker
Waste cotton yarn
Tapestry needle
Washable toy filling
Oddments of black, blue, and white tapestry wool for embroidery
^{5}/$_8$ x 10in (1.5 x 26cm) of blue craft felt

Gauge (Tension)
25 sts and 36 rows to 4in (10cm) over st st using US 5 (3.75mm) needles

Abbreviations
See page 126

Knit 7 rounds.

Round 39: K10, k2tog, k2 on first/third needle, k2, skpo, k10 on second/fourth needle. (13 sts on each needle)

Knit 7 rounds.

Round 47: K9, k2tog, k2 on first/third needle, k2, skpo, k9 on second/fourth needle. (12 sts on each needle)

Knit 2 rounds.

Round 50: K11, M1L, k1 on first/third needle, k1, M1R, k11 on second/fourth needle. (13 sts on each needle)

Knit 1 round.

Round 52: K12, M1L, k1 on first/third needle, k1, M1R, k12 on second/fourth needle. (14 sts on each needle)

Knit 1 round.

First leg

Using only four of the five double-pointed needles, rearrange the sts as follows:

Round 54: K21, put the next 21 sts onto a length of waste yarn, put the following 21 sts on a second length of waste yarn (the last 7 of these sts were knitted at the beg of the round), cast on 1 st.

Working clockwise, thread a short length of waste yarn through the st loop before the cast-on st and rep with a second length of waste yarn through the st after the cast-on st. The st after the cast-on st is the start of the round for First Leg only. (15 sts)

Arrange sts evenly over three double-pointed needles.

Knit 5 rounds.

Round 60: [K1, k2tog] five times. (10 sts in total)

Knit 1 round.

Cut A 4in (10cm) from last stitch on needle and thread into a tapestry needle. Pass tapestry needle through all the stitches on the needles in the order they would have been knitted, use the tip of the needle to pull the yarn at the point just after it has passed through the first stitch to draw the stitches tight to the yarn, then pull the yarn tight as it emerges through the last stitch. Secure the end.

Second leg

With the First Leg to the right, transfer the first 7 sts from the first length of waste yarn and the last 7 sts from the second length of waste yarn onto two separate double-pointed needles.

Round 54: Using a third needle, pick up 1 st through first marked st of the First Leg, k5, using a fourth needle, k2, cast on 1 st, k2, using needle that has now become free k5, pick up 1 st through second marked st of the First Leg then pick up one st through the cast on stitch of the First Leg. (6 sts on first needle, 5 sts on second, 7 sts on third)

As for First Leg, thread short lengths of waste yarn through the st loops before the cast-on st and after the cast-on st created on this round.

Round 55: K2tog, k4 on first needle, k5 on second needle, k4, k2tog, k1 on third needle. (5 sts on first and second needles, 6 sts on third)

Knit 4 rounds.

Round 60: K2tog, [k2tog, k1] four times, k2tog. (10 sts in total)

Knit 1 round.

As for the First Leg, cut A 4in (10cm) from the needle, thread a tapestry needle and pass this through the rem sts, starting with the first st of the round, and draw tight.

Third leg

Work as for Second Leg.

Fourth leg

With the Third Leg to the right, transfer the first 7 sts from the first length of waste yarn and the last 7 sts from the second length of waste yarn onto two separate double-pointed needles.

Round 54: Using a third needle, pick up 1 st through the first marked st of the third leg, k5, using a fourth needle, k5, using the needle that has now become free k4, pick up 1 st through the second marked st of the third leg then pick up one st through the cast-on stitch of the third leg. (6 sts on first needle, 5 sts on second, 6 sts on third)

Round 55: K2tog, k4 on first needle, k5 on second needle, k3, k2tog, k1 on third needle. (5 sts on each needle)

Knit 4 rounds.

Round 60: [K1, k2tog] five times. (10 sts in total)

Knit 1 round.

As for the First Leg, cut A 4in (10cm) from the needle, thread a tapestry needle and pass this through the rem sts, starting with the first st of the round, and draw tight.

First ear

With the center back to the right, arrange the sts as follows onto four double-pointed needles: transfer 7 sts from the waste yarn onto the first needle, 7 sts onto the second needle, 7 sts onto the third needle and 1 st onto the fourth needle. Join A to the first st of the first needle.

Round 24: K7 on each of the first three needles, k1, pick up 1 st from the nearest body st, pick up 1 st in each of the 4 cast-on sts, pick up 1 st from the next body st for the fourth needle. (7 sts on each needle)

Knit 6 rounds.

Round 31: K7 on each of the first three needles, k1, k2tog, k1, skpo, k1 on the fourth needle. (7 sts on each of first three needles, 5 sts on fourth)

Knit 1 round.

Round 33: Skpo, k5 on first needle, k7 on second needle, k5, k2tog on third needle, k5 on fourth needle. (6 sts on first needle, 7 sts on second, 6 sts on third, 5 sts on fourth)

Knit 1 round.

Round 35: Skpo, k4 on first needle, k7 on second needle, k4, k2tog on third needle, k5 on fourth needle. (5 sts on first needle, 7 sts on second 5 sts on third and fourth)

Knit 1 round.

Round 37: Skpo, k3 on first needle, k7 on second needle, k3, k2tog on third needle, k5 on fourth needle. (4 sts on first needle, 7 sts

on second, 4 sts on third, 5 sts on fourth)
Knit 1 round.

Round 39: Skpo, k2 on first needle, k7 on
second needle, k2, k2tog on third needle, k5
on fourth needle. (3 sts on first
needle, 7 sts on second, 3 sts on third,
5 sts on fourth)
Discard one needle and rearrange sts so
that there are 6 sts on each needle.
Knit 21 rounds.

Round 61: [K1, k2tog] six times.
(12 sts in total)
Knit 1 round.

Round 63: [K1, k2tog] four times.
(8 sts in total)
Knit 1 round.
As for First Leg, cut A 4in (10cm) from the
needle, thread a tapestry needle and pass
this through the rem sts, starting with
the first st of the round, and draw tight.

Second ear
With the First Ear to the right and the front
facing, work as for First Ear.

NOSE
Using US 5 (3.75mm) needles, the thumb
method, and B, cast on 7 sts.
Row 1 (WS): Purl.
Row 2: Knit.
Row 3: Purl.
Row 4: K1, M1R, k to last st, M1L, k1.
(9 sts)
Rows 5–7: Work in st st.
Rep rows 4–7 three more times. (15 sts)
Row 20: K1, M1R, k to last st, M1L, k1.
(17 sts)
Row 21: Purl.
Row 22: K1, M1R, k6, s2tog, k1, psso, k6,
M1L, k1.
Row 23: Purl.
Row 24: K1, M1R, k7, sl1 k7, M1L, k1.
(19 sts)
Row 25: Purl.
Row 26: K1, M1R, k7, s2tog, k1, psso, k7,
M1L, k1.

Row 27: Purl.
Row 28: K1, M1R, k8, sl1 k8, M1L, k1.
(21 sts)
Row 29: Purl.
Row 30: K9, s2tog, k1, psso, k9. (19 sts)
Row 31: Purl.
Row 32: K9, sl1, k9.
Row 33: Purl.
Row 34: K8, s2tog, k1, psso, k8. (17 sts)
Row 35: Purl.
Row 36: K7, s2tog, k1, psso, k7. (15 sts)
Row 37: Purl.
Bind (cast) off 5 sts, s2tog, k1, psso, pass
the st furthest from the tip on the right-hand
needle over the st nearest the tip, cont to
bind (cast) off to the end of the row.
Fasten off.

FINISHING
Press pieces gently following directions on
the yarn wrapper.
Weave the loose ends into the WS of the
body, insert toy filling, and sew opening
closed using mattress stitch.

Following the photograph for position, pin
the nose to the front. Using mattress stitch
and leaving an opening, sew the nose to the
body around the outer edge, insert toy filling,
and sew opening closed.
Embroider as follows:
The face: for each eye, using black tapestry
wool and backstitch, embroider an oval with
a vertical line either side of the iris area. Fill
in the irises with satin stitch in blue and the
areas on either side with satin stitch in white;
for the nose, using black and satin stitch,
embroider an inverted triangle. See also
page 124.
Cut the felt to fit around Albert's neck and
sew the ends of the collar together around
his neck.

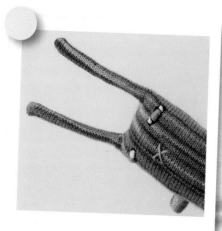

*Humphrey would love to be a prince or even a king!
He adores relaxing and getting things done for him.
Sometimes he dresses up in front of the mirror with
a pretend crown he's made out of cardboard!*

Humphrey Hare

pattern

Size
Completed creature measures approx.
15in (37cm) tall, including ears.

Yarn suggestion
Fine-weight yarn (such as Lion Brand
Sock Ease) 1 x 3½oz (100g) ball in
variegated grey/brown/yellow—Rock
Candy 201
Fine-weight yarn (such as Rowan Pure
Wool 4 ply) small amount in C (cream—
Snow 412)

Needles
Pair of US 1 (2.25mm) knitting needles

Extras
Tapestry needle
Washable toy filling
Oddments of black, blue, white, and
pink tapestry wool for embroidery

Gauge (Tension)
34 sts and 48 rows to 4in (10cm) over
st st using US 1 (2.25mm) needles.

Abbreviations
See page 126

BODY, LEGS, and EARS
Note: *this section is knitted sideways in one
piece, starting at center back.*
Using the cable method, cast on 60 sts.
Row 1 (RS): Knit.
Row 2: Purl.
Shape leg
*****Row 3:** Cast on 33 sts, k to end. (93 sts)
Row 4: Purl.
Row 5: Cast on 3 sts, k to end. (96 sts)
Row 6: Purl.
Rep rows 5–6 once more. (99 sts)
Starting with a k row, work 3 rows st st.
Shape ear
Row 12: Cast on 30 sts, p to end. (129 sts)
Starting with a k row, work 4 rows st st.
Row 17: Bind (cast) off 3 sts, k to end.
(126 sts)
Row 18: Purl.
Rep rows 17–18 once more. (123 sts)
Row 21: Cast on 3 sts, k to end. (126 sts)
Row 22: Purl.
Rep rows 21–22 once more. (129 sts)
Starting with a k row, work 3 rows st st.
Row 28: Bind (cast) off 30 sts, p to end.
(99 sts)
Starting with a k row, work 4 rows st st.
Row 33: Bind (cast) off 3 sts, k to end.
(96 sts)
Row 34: Purl.
Rep rows 33–34 once more. (93 sts)
Row 37: Bind (cast) off 33 sts, k to end.
(60 sts)*
Starting with a p row, work 3 rows st st.
Rep from * to *.

Starting with a p row, work 2 rows st st.
Bind (cast) off.

ARMS (make two)
Cast on 18 sts.
Starting with a k row, work 8 rows st st.
Bind (cast) off.

FINISHING
Press knitted pieces following instructions on
the yarn wrapper. Using mattress stitch, sew
first cast-on and last bound-off edges together
for center back seam. With seam at center
back, sew seam from top of one ear, down
ear, across top of head, up second ear, and
across top of second ear. Insert toy filling into
head—but do not stuff ears—and body
through open legs, then sew up leg seams
from side of one foot, around foot, up first leg,
down second leg, and around second foot,
inserting toy filling into legs as you sew the
seam. Fold each arm in half, matching row
ends. Using mattress stitch, sew cast-on
edges then bound-off edges together. Insert
toy filling. Using chain stitch or mattress stitch
as preferred, sew arms to sides of body. Using
C, make a pompom approx. 2in (5cm) in
diameter and sew to back above legs.
Embroider as follows: The face: for each eye,
using black tapestry wool and backstitch, embroider an oval with a vertical line either side of
the iris area. Fill in the irises with satin stitch in
blue and the areas on either side with satin
stitch in white; for the mouth, using pink,
embroider a cross. See also page 124.

Rita Raccoon is a workaholic; she is always checking her emails and talking on her phone, as well as looking after her two mischievous boys. Sometimes she is so busy she freezes on the spot for a few minutes—until she's off again!

Rita Raccoon

pattern

FRONT

First leg

*Using the thumb method and A, cast on 5 sts.

Row 1 and every alt row (WS): Purl.

Row 2: K1, M1R, k3, M1L, k1. (7 sts)

Row 4: K1, M1R, k5, M1L, k1. (9 sts)

Row 5: Purl.

Row 6: Knit.

Row 7: Purl.*

Row 8: K1, M1R, k to end. (10 sts)

Rows 9: Purl.

Cut yarn and put sts onto a stitch holder.

Second leg

Work as for First Leg from * to *.

Row 8: K to last st, M1L, k1. (10 sts)

Row 9: Purl.

Leave sts on needle.

Join legs

Row 10 (RS): Knit across 10 sts on needle, cast on 12 sts using the backward loop method, with RS facing knit across 10 sts from stitch holder. (32 sts)

Row 15: P9, p2tog, p10, p2togtbl, p9. (30 sts)

Starting with a k row, work 26 rows st st.

Shape arms

Row 42: K1, M1R, k to last st, M1L, k1. (32 sts)

Row 43: P1, M1L, p to last st, M1R, p1. (34 sts)

Rep rows 42–43 once more. (38 sts)

Starting with a k row, work 2 rows st st.

Row 48: K1, skpo, k to last 3 sts, k2tog, k1. (36 sts)

Row 49: P1, p2tog, p to last 3 sts, p2togtbl, p1. (34 sts)

Rep rows 48–49 once more. (30 sts)

Starting with a k row, work 8 rows st st.

Head

Join in B.

Using B, starting with a k row and stranding A up the WS right-hand edge, work 4 rows st st,

Cut B and cont in A.

Starting with a k row, work 6 rows st st.

Shape first ear

Row 70: K15, turn.

Work on this set of 15 sts only and put the rem sts on a stitch holder.

Rows 71: P1, p2tog, p to end. (14 sts)

Row 72: K to last 3 sts, k2tog, k1. (13 sts)

Rep rows 71–72 four more times. (5 sts)

Row 81: Purl.

Bind (cast) off.

Shape second ear

Put the 15 sts on stitch holder onto a needle and with RS facing, rejoin yarn.

Row 70: K15.

Rows 71: P to last 3 sts, p2togtbl, p1. (14 sts)

Size

Completed creature measures approx. 9in (23cm) tall

Yarn suggestion

Lightweight yarn (such as Rowan Wool Cotton) 1 x 1³/₄oz (50g) ball in A (black—Inky 908) and 1 ball in B (cream—Antique 900)

Needles

Pair of US 3 (3.25mm) needles

Extras

Stitch holder

Tapestry needle

Washable toy filling

Oddments of black and blue tapestry wool for embroidery

Gauge (Tension)

23 sts and 35 rows to 4in (10cm) over st st using US 3 (3.25mm) needles

Abbreviations

See page 126

Row 72: K1, skpo, k to end. (13 sts)
Rep rows 71–72 four times. (5 sts)
Row 81: Purl.
Bind (cast) off.

BACK

Work as given for Front, using A only.

TAIL (make two)

Using the thumb method and A, cast on
10 sts.
Starting with a k row, work 4 rows st st.
Join in B, strand the yarn not in use up the
WS right-hand edge of the work.
Using B.
Starting with a k row, work 2 rows st st.
Row 7: K1, M1R, k to last st,
M1L, k1. (12 sts)
Row 8: Purl.
Rep rows 1–8 eight more

times. (28 sts) Using A.
Starting with a k row, work 4 rows st st.
Using B.
Starting with a k row, work 4 rows st st.
Using A.
Starting with a k row, work 4 rows st st.
Using B.
Starting with a k row, work 4 rows st st.
Using A.
Row 89: K1, skpo, k to last 3 sts, k2tog, k1.
(26 sts)
Row 90: Purl.
Rep rows 89–90 once more. (24 sts)
Using B.
Row 93: As row 89. (22 sts)
Row 94: P1, p2tog, p to last
3 sts, p2togtbl, p1. (20 sts)
Rep rows 93–94 once more.
(16 sts)
Cut B and cont in A.
Row 97: As row 89. (14 sts)
Row 98: Purl.
Bind (cast) off.

NOSE

Using the thumb method and A,
cast on 28 sts.
Row 1 and every alt row (WS): Purl.
Row 2: K24, short-row-wrap the next
st, turn.
Row 4: K20, short-row-wrap the next
st, turn.
Row 6: K16, short-row-wrap the next
st, turn.
Row 8: K12, short-row-wrap the next
st, turn.
Row 10: K8, short-row-wrap the next
st, turn.
Row 12: K4, short-row-wrap the next
st, turn.
Row 14: K4, [pick up the short-row-wrap
and k tog with the wrapped st, k3] six times.
Rows 15–42: Rep rows 1–14, twice.
Bind (cast) off.

FINISHING

Press pieces gently following directions on
the yarn wrapper.
Using mattress stitch, sew cast-on and
bound-off edges of nose together. Insert toy
filling into nose. Using mattress stitch, sew
nose to front of head, following photograph
for position.
Using mattress stitch, sew the body pieces
together around the outer edges, weaving
loose ends into seam wherever possible,
and leaving a small opening. Insert toy filling
and sew opening closed.
Using mattress stitch, sew tail pieces
together around the outer edges, leaving
the cast-on edges open. Weave in loose
ends, insert toy filling, and sew cast-on
edge to back body piece, centered just
above the legs.
Embroider as follows:
The face: for each eye, working on the white
band and using black tapestry wool and
backstitch, embroider an oval with a
vertical line either side of the iris area. Fill in
the irises with satin stitch in blue; for the
nose, using black and satin stitch,
embroider over the tip of the knitted nose.
See also page 124.

Percy is a distinguished sort of dog; he sniffs out the finest sausages and never settles for anything other than the best. His favorite sausage at the moment is pork and marmalade. Delicious!

Percival Long Dog

Size

Completed creature measures approx. 37in (93cm) long

Yarn suggestion

Heavyweight yarn (such as Lang Yarns West) 2 x 1³/₄oz (50g) balls in variegated orange/brown—732.0059

Needles

Pair of US 6 (4mm) knitting needles

Extras

Tapestry needle

Washable toy filling

Oddments of black and white tapestry wool for embroidery

Gauge (Tension)

19 sts and 26 rows to 4in (10cm) over st st using US 6 (4mm) needles

Abbreviations

See page 126

pattern

BODY, HEAD, and LEGS

Using the cable method, cast on 53 sts.

Row 1 (RS): Knit.

Row 2: Purl.

Shape tail and first back leg

Row 3: Cast on 8 sts, k34, M1R, k1, M1L, k26. (63 sts)

Row 4: Cast on 8 sts, p to end. (71 sts)

Row 5: K2, M1R, k31, skpo, k1, k2tog, k31, M1L, k2. (71 sts)

Row 6: P33, p2tog, p1, p2togtbl, p33. (69 sts)

Row 7: K2, M1R, k30, skpo, k1, k2tog, k30, M1L, k2. (69 sts)

Row 8: P32, p2tog, p1, p2togtbl, p32. (67 sts)

Row 9: K2, skpo, k27, skpo, k1, k2tog, k27, k2tog, k2. (63 sts)

Row 10: P29, p2tog, p1, p2togtbl, p29. (61 sts)

Row 11: K2, skpo, k to last 4 sts, k2tog, k2. (59 sts)

Row 12: Purl.

Row 13: Bind (cast) off 8 sts, k to end. (51 sts)

Row 14: Bind (cast) off 8 sts, p to end. (43 sts)

Starting with a k row, work 4 rows st st.

Shape second back leg

Row 19: Cast on 8 sts, k to end. (51 sts)

Row 20: Cast on 8 sts, p to end. (59 sts)

Row 21: K2, M1R, k to last 2 sts, M1L, k2. (61 sts)

Row 22: Purl.

Rep rows 21–22 once more. (63 sts)

Row 25: K2, skpo, k to last 4 sts, k2tog, k2. (61 sts)

Row 26: Purl.

Rep rows 25–26 once more. (59 sts)

Row 29: Bind (cast) off 8 sts, k to end. (51 sts)

Row 30: Bind (cast) off 8 sts, p to end. (43 sts)

Body

Starting with a k row, work in st st until work measures 30in (76cm) from cast-on edge, ending with a WS row.

Shape head and first front leg

Next row: Cast on 8 sts, k to end. (51 sts)

Next row: Cast on 8 sts, p to end. (59 sts)

Next row: K2, M1R, k27, M1R, k1, M1L, k27, M1L, k2. (63 sts)

Next row and foll 3 alt rows: Purl.

Next row: K2, M1R, k28, M1R, k3, M1L,

k28, M1L, k2. (67 sts)
Next row: K2, skpo, k28, M1R, k3, M1L, k28, k2tog, k2. (67 sts)
Next row: K2, skpo, k28, M1R, k3, M1L, k28, k2tog, k2. (67 sts)
Next row: Bind (cast) off 8 sts, k23, M1R, k3, M1L, k32. (61 sts)
Next row: Bind (cast) off 8 sts, p to end. (53 sts)
Next row: K25, M1R, k3, M1L, k25. (55 sts)
Starting with a p row, work 3 rows st st.

Shape head and second front leg
Next row: Cast on 8 sts, k to end. (63 sts)
Next row: Cast on 8 sts, p to end. (71 sts)
Next row: K2, M1R, k30, skpo, k3, k2tog, k30, M1L, k2. (71 sts)
Next row and foll 3 alt rows: Purl.
Next row: K2, M1R, k30, skpo, k3, k2tog, k30, M1L, k2. (71 sts)
Next row: K2, skpo, k28, skpo, k3, k2tog, k28, k2tog, k2. (67 sts)
Next row: K2, skpo, k26, skpo, k3, k2tog, k26, k2tog, k2. (63 sts)
Bind (cast) off 8 sts, k20, skpo, k1, k2tog, k29. (53 sts)
Bind (cast) off 8 sts, p to end. (45 sts)
Next row: K2, skpo, k16, skpo, k1, k2tog, k16, k2tog, k2. (41 sts)
Next row: Purl.
Next row: K2, skpo, k2, skpo, k10, skpo, k1, k2tog, k10, k2tog, k2, k2tog, k2. (35 sts)
Next row: P2, p2tog, p to last 4 sts, p2togtbl, p2. (33 sts)

Next row: K2, skpo, k2, skpo, k6, skpo, k1, k2tog, k6, k2tog, k2, k2tog, k2. (27 sts)
Next row: P2, p2tog, p to last 4 sts, p2togtbl, p2. (25 sts)
Next row: K2, skpo, k6, skpo, k1, k2tog, k6, k2tog, k2. (21 sts)
Starting with a p row, work 9 rows st st.

Shape nose
Next row: K2, skpo, k4, skpo, k1, k2tog, k4, k2tog, k2. (17 sts)
Next row: P2, p2tog, p2, p2tog, p1, p2togtbl, p2, p2togtbl, p2. (13 sts)
Bind (cast) off.

EARS (both together)
Using thumb method, cast on 51 sts.
Row 1: [K1, p1] rep to last st, k1.
Row 1 establishes seed st.
Rep row 1 once more.
Row 3: [K1, p1] twice, k1, M1R, k to last 5 sts, M1L, [k1, p1] twice, k1. (53 sts)
Row 4: [K1, p1] twice, p to last 3 sts, k1, p1, k1.
Rep rows 3–4 once more. (55 sts)
Row 7: [K1, p1] twice, k1, skpo, k to last 7 sts, k2tog, [k1, p1] twice, k1. (53 sts)
Row 8: [K1, p1] twice, p to last 3 sts, k1, p1, k1.
Rep rows 7–8 once more. (51 sts)
Row 11: [K1, p1] rep to last st, k1.
Rep row 11 once more.
Bind (cast) off in seed st.

FINISHING
Press knitted pieces following instructions on the yarn wrapper.
Fold knitting in half lengthwise, matching legs. Pleat center of ears and sew to head, following photograph for position.
Using mattress stitch, sew body together along lower edges, weaving loose ends into the seam wherever possible. Insert toy filling as you sew.
Embroider as follows:
The face: for each eye, using black tapestry wool and backstitch, embroider an oval with a vertical line either side of the iris area. Fill in the irises with satin stitch in blue and the areas on either side with satin stitch in white; for the nose, using black and satin stitch, embroider an inverted triangle on the end of the knitted nose; for the moustache, using black and backstitch, embroider a curl on each cheek. See also page 124.

Size

Completed cupcake measures approx.
8in (20cm) tall

Yarn suggestion

Lightweight yarn (such as Rowan
Cotton Glacé) 1 x 1³/₄oz (50g) ball in
A (white—Bleached 726), 1 ball in
D (pink—Bubbles 724)

Lightweight yarn (such as Rowan Wool
Cotton) 1 x 1³/₄oz (50g) ball in
B (brown—Bronze 967), 1 ball in
C (pale pink—Tender 951)

Fine-weight yarn (such as Rowan
4 ply Soft) 1 x 1³/₄oz (50g) ball in E
(red—Honk 374)

Needles

Set of four double-pointed US 3 (3mm)
knitting needles

Extras

Round marker

Tapestry needle

Washable toy filling

Gauge (Tension)

25 sts and 33 rows to 4in (10cm) over
st st using US 3 (3mm) needles

Abbreviations

See page 126

Completely fat-free, this cupcake can definitely be snacked upon between meals. Frost it with yellow yarn if you prefer a lemon fancy or pink yarn for a strawberry parfait.

Giant Cupcake

pattern

CUPCAKE
Frosting
Using the thumb method and A, cast on 6 sts onto one needle.

Round 1 (RS): To start working in the round, slip half the stitches onto a second needle and position the two needles side by side with the first cast-on stitch and the last cast-on stitch adjacent on separate needles. Use a third needle to start knitting the round starting with the first cast-on stitch and working two stitches. Use a fourth needle to knit the next two stitches, one from each of the original two needles. (2 sts on each needle.) Complete knitting the round with the needle that has now become free. Place round marker at the start of the round.

Round 2: [Inc] six times.
(4 sts on each needle)
Round 3: Knit.
Round 4: [K1, M1R] twelve times.
(8 sts on each needle)
Round 5: Knit.
Round 6: [K2, M1R] twelve times.
(12 sts on each needle)
Round 7: Knit.
Round 8: [K3, M1R] twelve times.
(16 sts on each needle)
Rounds 9–10: Knit.
Round 11: [K4, M1R] twelve times.
(20 sts on each needle)
Rounds 12–13: Knit.

Round 14: [K5, M1R] twelve times.
(24 sts on each needle)
Knit 4 rounds.
Cut A and join in B.
Cake
Knit 20 rounds.
Round 39: [K4, skpo, k4, k2tog] six times.
(20 sts on each needle)
Cut B and join in C and D.
Case
Round 40: [K1C, k1D] rep to end of round.
Rep round 40 twenty-three more times.
Using D, knit 2 rounds.
Cut D.
Base
Work in C only.
Purl 3 rounds.
Weave in loose ends and insert toy filling.
Round 69: [K3, k2tog] twelve times.
(16 sts on each needle)
Round 70: Purl.
Round 71: Knit.
Round 72: Purl.
Round 73: [K2, k2tog] twelve times.
(12 sts on each needle)
Round 74: Purl.
Round 75: Knit.
Round 76: Purl.
Insert toy filling.
Round 77: [K1, k2tog] twelve times.
(8 sts on each needle)
Round 78: Purl.

Round 79: Knit.
Round 80: Purl.
Round 81: [K2tog] twelve times.
(4 sts on each needle)
Round 82: Purl.
Cut C 4in (10cm) from the last stitch on the needle and thread onto a tapestry needle. Pass the tapestry needle through all the stitches on the needles in the order they would have been knitted, use the tip of the needle to pull the yarn at the point just after it has passed through the first stitch to draw the stitches tight to the yarn, then pull the yarn tight as it emerges through the last stitch. Secure the end.

CHERRY
Using the thumb method and E, cast on 12 sts.
Row 1 (WS): Purl.
Row 2: Knit.
Rows 3-16: Rep rows 1–2 seven times or until the knitted piece is a square.
Bind (cast) off.

FINISHING
Form the cherry by working a line of running stitches around the four sides of the square piece, placing some toy filling in the center, drawing the stitches up tight and securing the end. Sew the cherry to the top of the cupcake.

Mimi Mushroom is by far the best at hide-and-seek among the trees. She is small and quiet and can stay still for a long time.

Mimi Mushroom

pattern

FRONT

First leg

Using the thumb method, cast on 5 sts.

Row 1 (WS): Purl.

Row 2: K1, M1R, k to end. (6 sts)

Row 3: Purl.

Rep rows 2–3 three more times. (9 sts)

Row 10: K1, M1R, k5, k2tog, k1. (9 sts)

Row 11: Purl.

Row 12: As row 10.

Row 13. Purl.

Cut yarn and put sts onto stitch holder.

Second leg

Using the thumb method, cast on 5 sts.

Row 1 (WS): Purl.

Row 2: K1, M1R, k3, M1L, k1. (7 sts)

Row 3: Purl.

Row 4: Knit.

Row 5: Purl.

Leave sts on needle and do not cut yarn.

Join legs

Row 14: Knit across 7 sts on needles, cast on 3 sts using the backward loop method, with RS facing knit across 6 sts from stitch holder, k2tog, k1. (18 sts)

Body

Row 15: P7, p2tog, p1, p2togtbl, p6. (16 sts)

Starting with a k row, work 9 rows st st.

Skirt ridge

Rows 25–27: Knit.

Starting with a k row, work 10 rows st st.

Shape arms

Row 38: K1, M1R, k to end. (17 sts)

Row 39: Cast on 2 sts using the backward loop method, p to end. (19 sts)

Row 40: Knit.

Row 41: P1, M1L, p to end. (20 sts)

Row 42: K1, M1R, k to end. (21 sts)

Row 43: P1, p2tog, p to last st, M1R, p1.

Row 44: K1, M1R, k to end. (22 sts)

Row 45: Bind (cast) off 2 sts, p to end. (20 sts)

Row 46: K1, skpo, k to last 3 sts, k2tog, k1. (18 sts)

Row 47: Purl.

Row 48: K1, skpo, k to end. (17 sts)

Row 49: Purl.

Row 50: K1, skpo, k to last st, M1L, k1.

Row 51: Purl.

Row 52: K to last st, M1L, K1. (18 sts)

Rep rows 51–52 once more. (19 sts)

Row 55: Purl.

Row 56: K1, M1R, k to last st, M1L, k1. (21 sts)

Rep rows 55–56 once more. (23 sts)

Shape top

Row 59: Cast on 4 sts using the backward loop method, p to end. (27 sts)

Row 60: Cast on 7 sts using the backward loop method, k to end. (34 sts)

Row 61: Purl.

Row 62: K1, skpo, k to end. (33 sts)

Row 63: Purl.

Row 64: Knit.

Row 65: Purl.

Row 66: K1, skpo, k to end. (32 sts)

Starting with a p row, work 3 rows st st.

Row 70: K1, skpo, k to last 3 sts, k2tog, k1. (30 sts)

Row 71: Purl.

Row 72: K to last 3 sts, k2tog, k1. (29 sts)

Row 73: Purl.

Rep rows 70–73 twice more. (23 sts)

Row 82: K1, skpo, k to last 3 sts, k2tog, k1. (21 sts)

Row 83: Purl.

Rep rows 82–83 once more. (19 sts)

Row 86: K1, skpo, k to last 3 sts, k2tog, k1. (17 sts)

Row 87: P1, p2tog, p to last 3 sts, p2togtbl, p1. (15 sts)

Rep rows 86–87 once more. (11 sts)

Bind (cast) off.

BACK

Work as given for Front, reversing RS of work (to make a mirrored pair of pieces) by reading knit for purl and vice versa. See page 118 for reverse shaping tips.

FINISHING

Press pieces gently following directions on the yarn wrapper.

Using mattress stitch, sew body pieces together around the outer edges, leaving a small opening. Insert toy filling and sew opening closed.

Embroider as follows:

The face: for each eye, using black tapestry wool and backstitch, embroider an oval. Using satin stitch, embroider a wide black central stripe for the irises and fill in the areas on either side with satin stitch in white; for the eyebrows, using black and backstitch, embroider a line above each eye; for the mouth, using black and backstitch, embroider the opening and outline the teeth. Fill in the mouth with satin stitch in orange. For the cheeks, using backstitch and orange, embroider circles. See also page 124.

Size

Completed creature measures approx.
9 in (23cm) tall

Yarn suggestion

Lightweight yarn (such as Debbie
Bliss Prima) 1 x 1³⁄₄oz (50g) ball in
sand—35705

Needles

Pair of US 3 (3.25mm) knitting needles

Extras

One stitch holder

Tapestry needle

Washable toy filling

Oddments of black, white, and orange
tapestry wool for embroidery

Gauge (Tension)

26 sts and 37 rows to 4in (10cm) over
st st using US 3 (3.25mm) needles

Abbreviations

See page 126

Robin is a soft and gentle bird. He teaches sky-diving to beginners but has to watch his weight because he is partial to a worm or two!

Size

Completed creature measures approx. 6¾in (17cm) tall, excluding legs

Yarn suggestion

Lightweight yarn (such as Debbie Bliss Rialto) 1 x 1¾oz (50g) ball in A (red —12), 1 ball in B (brown—05), and 1 ball in C (pink—13)

Needles

Pair of US 3 (3.25mm) knitting needles

Extras

Tapestry needle

Washable toy filling

Scrap of cream felt

Sewing needle and thread to match felt

Oddments of black, green, and white tapestry wool for embroidery

Gauge (Tension)

24 sts and 34 rows to 4in (10cm) over st st using US 3 (3.25mm) needles

Abbreviations

See page 126

Robin Red Breast

pattern

Note: decrease (dec) using k2tog if second stitch of two being worked together is a knit stitch or p2tog if it is a purl stitch.

FRONT

Using the cable method and A, cast on 30 sts.

Row 1 (RS): Knit.

Row 2: Purl.

Shape tummy

Row 3: K2, M1R, k to last 2 sts, M1L, k2. (32 sts)

Row 4: Purl.

Rep rows 3–4 five more times. (42 sts)

Starting with a k row, work 22 rows st st.

Bind (cast) off.

Shape head

Using B, pick up 42 sts across bound-off edge.

Next row: Purl.

***Next row:** [P2, k2] rep to last 2 sts, p2.

Next row: [K2, p2] rep to last 2 sts, k2.

Rep last 2 rows three more times.

Next row: [P2, k2] rep to last 2 sts, p2.

Next row: Dec, rib as set to last 2 sts, dec. (40 sts)

Rib 3 rows as set.

Rep last 4 rows once more. (38 sts)

Next row: Dec, rib as set to last 2 sts, dec. (36 sts)

Rib 1 row as set.

Rep last 2 rows three more times. (30 sts)

Next row: Dec, rib as set to last 2 sts, dec.

Rep last row five more times. (18 sts)

Bind (cast) off.*

BACK

Using the cable method and B, cast on 30 sts.

Row 1 (RS): [K2, p2] rep to last 2 sts, k2.

Row 2: [P2, k2] rep to last 2 sts, p2.

Row 3: Cast on 2 sts, [p2, k2] rep to end. (32 sts)

Row 4: Cast on 2 sts, [k2, p2] rep to last 2 sts, k2. (34 sts)

Row 5: [P2, k2] rep to last 2 sts, p2.

Row 6: [K2, p2] rep to last 2 sts, k2.

Row 7: Cast on 2 sts, [k2, p2] rep to end. (36 sts)

Row 8: Cast on 2 sts, [p2, k2] rep to last 2 sts, p2. (38 sts)

Row 9: [K2, p2] rep to last 2 sts, k2.

Row 10: [P2, k2] rep to last 2 sts, p2.

Row 11: Cast on 3 sts, p3, [k2, p2] rep to last 2 sts, k2. (41 sts)

Row 12: Cast on 3 sts, k3, [p2, k2] rep to last 5 sts, p2, k3. (44 sts)

Row 13: P3, [k2, p2] rep to last 5 sts, k2, p3.

Row 14: K3, [p2, k2] rep to last 5 sts, p2, k3.

Rep rows 13–14 ten more times.

Row 35: As row 13.

Row 36: Dec, k1, [p2, k2] rep to last 5 sts, p2, k1, dec. (42 sts)

Rep from * to * of Front.

WINGS (make two)

Using the thumb method and B, cast on 9 sts.

Row 1 (WS): [K1, p1] rep to last st , k1.

Rep row 1 twice more.

Row 4: K1, p1, k1, M1R, k to last 3 sts, M1L, k1, p1, k1. (11 sts)

Row 5: K1, p to last st, k1.

Rep rows 4–5 twice more. (15 sts)

Row 10: K1, p1, k to last 2 sts, p1, k1.

Row 11: K1, p to last st, k1.

Rep rows 10–11 five more times.

Row 22: K1, p1, k1, skpo, k to last 5 sts, k2tog, k1, p1, k1. (13 sts)

Row 23: K1, p to last st, k1.

Rep rows 22–23 twice more. (9 sts)

Row 28: K1, p1, k1, s2tog, k1, psso, k1, p1, k1. (7 sts)

Row 29: K1, p to last st, k1.

Row 30: K1, p1, s2tog, k1, psso, p1, k1. (5 sts)

Row 31: [K1, p1] twice, k1.

Rep row 31 twice more.

Row 34: K1, p3tog, k1. (3 sts)

Row 35: K1, p1, k1.

Rep row 35 four more times.

Cut yarn leaving a long tail. Pass yarn through rem 3 sts and pull up tight.

FEET (make two)

Using the cable method and C, cast on 18 sts.

*Bind (cast) off 5 sts, slip st on right-hand needle onto left-hand needle.

Cast on 5 sts.*

Rep from * to *.

Bind (cast) off 18 sts.

WORM (optional)

Using the cable method and C, cast on 40 sts loosely.

Bind (cast) off all sts tightly.

FINISHING

Press knitted pieces following instructions on yarn wrapper. Weave in loose ends neatly. Using mattress stitch and working one stitch in from the edge, sew body pieces together around the outer edges, leaving a small opening. Insert toy filling and sew opening closed. Sew legs to lower edge of body, following photograph for position. Position cast-on edge of each wing at an angle on sides of body. Using slip stitch, sew front and top edges of wings to body, leaving wings tips free. Bend wings up.

Cut felt into a diamond, fold in half and position on face for beak. Using sewing needle and thread, sew across middle of diamond to sew to head. Sew worm into beak. Embroider as follows:

The face: for each eye, using black tapestry wool and backstitch, embroider an oval with a vertical line either side of the iris area. Fill in the irises with satin stitch in green and the areas on either side with satin stitch in white. See also page 124.

Deirdre is by far the most glamorous of the creatures. Her favorite pastime is shopping for new wings; she always goes to designer wing shops and picks out pairs in this season's colors.

Deidre Dragonfly

pattern

Note: to prepare for beading, thread sewing cotton through a fine needle and tie to A, then pass the needle through the beads and slide them down the yarn.

BODY and HEAD
Tail
Using four US 3 (3mm) double-pointed needles, the thumb method, and A, cast on 6 sts onto one needle.

Round 1 (RS): To start working in the round, slip half the stitches onto a second needle and position the two needles side by side with the first cast-on stitch and the last cast-on stitch adjacent on separate needles. Use a third needle to start knitting the round starting with the first cast-on stitch and working two stitches. Use a fourth needle to knit the next two stitches, one from each of the original two needles. (2 sts on each needle.) Complete knitting the round with the needle that has now become free.

Round 2: [Inc] six times.
(4 sts on each needle)
Arrange sts over four needles.
(3 sts on each needle)
Place round marker at the start of the round. Starting with a knit (RS) round, place beads as indicated by the chart. The first and third needles hold the side stitches, the second and fourth needles hold the front and back

stitches—those on which beading and shaping occur. Work shaping as follows:
Rounds 3–4 (RS): Knit 2 rounds.
Round 5: K3 on first/third needle, k1, M1R, k1, M1L, k1 on second/fourth needle. (3 sts on first needle, 5 sts on second, 3 sts on third, 5 sts on fourth)
Rounds 6–7: Knit 2 rounds.
Round 8: K3 on first/third needle, work as chart as follows: k1, M1R, k1, PB, k1, M1L, k1 on second/fourth needle. (3 sts on first needle, 7 sts on second, 3 sts on third, 7 sts on fourth)
Round 9: Knit one round.
Round 10: K3 on first/third needle, work as chart as follows: k1, PB, k3, PB, k1 on second/fourth needle.
Cont beading as indicated by chart on the second and fourth needles.
Rounds 11–44: Knit 34 rounds.
Round 45: K3 on first/third needle, k1, M1R, k1, PB, k1, PB, k1, M1L, k1 on second/fourth needle. (3 sts on first needle, 9 sts on second, 3 sts on third, 9 sts on fourth)
Rounds 46–86: Knit 41 rounds.
Round 87: K3 on first/third needle, k1, M1R, PB, k5, PB, M1L, k1 on second/fourth needle. (3 sts on first needle, 11 sts on second, 3 sts on third, 11 sts on fourth)

Size
Completed creature measures approx. 16in (40cm) long

Yarn suggestion
Lightweight yarn (such as Debbie Bliss Baby Cashmerino) 1 x 1³/₄oz (50g) ball in A (green—340016) and 1 ball in B (gold—340025)

Bead suggestion
¹/₄in (4mm) round beads (such as Miracle Bead) 238 iridescent purple beads

Needles
Set of five double-pointed US 3 (3mm) knitting needles
Pair of US 3 (3mm) knitting needles

Extras
Round marker
Waste cotton yarn
Tapestry needle
Washable toy filling
Oddments of black, blue, and white tapestry wool for embroidery

Gauge (Tension)
26 sts and 46 rows to 4in (10cm) over st st using US 3 (3mm) needles

Abbreviations
See page 126

Rounds 88–122: Knit 35 rounds.
Insert toy filling.

Round 123: K3 on first/third needle, k1, skpo, k5, k2tog, k1 on second/fourth needle. (3 sts on first needle, 9 sts on second, 3 sts on third, 9 sts on fourth)

Rounds 124–126: Knit 3 rounds.

Round 127: K3 on first/third needle, k1, skpo, k3, k2tog, k1 on second/fourth needle. (3 sts on first needle, 7 sts on second, 3 sts on third, 7 sts on fourth)

Rounds 128–132: Knit 5 rounds.

Round 133: K3 on first/third needle, k1, skpo, PB, k2tog, k1 on second/fourth needle. (3 sts on first needle, 5 sts on second, 3 sts on third, 5 sts on fourth)

Round 134: Knit one round.
Chart completed.
Insert toy filling.

Head

Rounds 135–136: Knit 2 rounds.

Round 137: K3 on first/third needle, k1, M1R, k3, M1L, k1 on second/fourth needle. (3 sts on first needle, 7 sts on second, 3 sts on third, 7 sts on fourth)

Round 138: K3 on first/third needle, k1, M1R, k5, M1L, k1 on second/fourth needle. (3 sts on first needle, 9 sts on second, 3 sts on third, 9 sts on fourth)

Rounds 139–140: Knit 2 rounds.

Round 141: K3 on first/third needle, k1, M1R, k7, M1L, k1 on second/fourth needle. (3 sts on first needle, 11 sts on second, 3 sts on third, 11 sts on fourth)

Rounds 142–152: Knit 11 rounds.

Round 153: K1, k2tog on first/third needle, k2, k2tog, k1, k2tog, k2, k2tog on second/fourth needle. (2 sts on first needle, 8 sts on second, 2 sts on third, 8 sts on fourth)

Rounds 154–155: Knit 2 rounds.
Insert toy filling.

Round 156: K2tog on first/third needle, [k2tog] four times on second/fourth needle. (1 sts on first needle, 4 sts on second, 1 sts on third, 4 sts on fourth)

Round 157: Knit 1 round.
Cut A 4in (10cm) from the last stitch on the needle and thread into a tapestry needle. Pass the tapestry needle through all the stitches on the needles in the order they would have been knitted, use the tip of the needle to pull the yarn at the point just after it has passed through the first stitch to draw the stitches tight to the yarn, then pull the yarn tight as it emerges through the last stitch. Secure the end.

LARGER WINGS (make two)

Using US 3 (3mm) needles, the thumb method, and B, cast on 10 sts.

Row 1: K1tbl, [p1, k1] four times, bring yarn forward between the needles, sl1 purlwise
Rep row 1 three more times.

Row 5: K1tbl, inc, [p1, k1] three times, inc, bring yarn forward between the needles, sl1 purlwise. (12 sts)

Row 6: K1tbl, inc, [p1, k1] four times, inc, bring yarn forward between the needles, sl1 purlwise. (14 sts)

Row 7: K1tbl, [k1, p1] six times, bring yarn forward between the needles, sl1 purlwise.

Row 8: K1tbl, inc, [k1, p1] five times, inc, bring yarn forward between the needles, sl1 purlwise. (16 sts)

Row 9: K1tbl, [p1, k1] seven times, bring yarn forward between the needles, sl1 purlwise.

Row 10: K1tbl, inc, [p1, k1] six times, inc, bring yarn forward between the needles, sl1 purlwise. (18 sts)

Row 11: K1tbl, [k1, p1] eight times, bring yarn forward between the needles, sl1 purlwise.

Row 12: K1tbl, [p1, k1] eight times, bring yarn forward between the needles, sl1 purlwise.

Row 13: Rep row 11.

Row 14: K1tbl, inc, [k1, p1] seven times, inc, bring yarn forward between the needles, sl1 purlwise. (20 sts)

Row 15: K1tbl, [p1, k1] nine times, bring yarn forward between the needles, sl1 purlwise.

Row 16: K1tbl, [k1, p1] nine times, bring yarn forward between the needles, sl1 purlwise.
Rep rows 15–16 nine more times.

Row 35: K1tbl, skpo, [p1, k1] seven times, k2tog, bring yarn forward between the needles, sl1 purlwise. (18 sts)

Row 36: K1tbl, skpo, [p1, k1] six times, k2tog, bring yarn forward between the needles, sl1 purlwise.
(16 sts)
Bind (cast) off as follows: Skpo, k1, pass the first st loop on the right-hand needle over the second, cont to bind off keeping the seed st patt correct until 2 sts rem on the left-hand needle, k2tog, pass the first st loop on the right-hand needle over the second.
Fasten off.

SMALLER WINGS (make two)

Using US 3 (3mm) needles, the thumb method, and B, cast on 10 sts.

Row 1: K1tbl, [p1, k1] four times, bring yarn forward between the needles, sl1 purlwise
Rep row 1 three more times.

Row 5: K1tbl, inc, [p1, k1] three times, inc, bring yarn forward between the needles, sl1 purlwise. (12 sts)

Row 6: K1tbl, [k1, p1] five times, bring yarn forward between the needles, sl1 purlwise.

Row 7: K1tbl, [p1, k1] five times, bring yarn forward between the needles, sl1 purlwise.
Rep rows 6–7 fourteen more times.

Row 36: K1tbl, skpo, [k1, p1] three times, k2tog, bring yarn forward between the needles, sl1 purlwise. (10 sts)
Bind (cast) off as follows: Skpo, p1, pass the first st loop on the right-hand needle over the second, cont to bind off keeping the seed st patt correct until 2 sts rem on the left-hand needle, k2tog, pass the first st loop on the right-hand needle over the second.
Fasten off.

FINISHING

Press pieces gently following directions on
the yarn wrapper.

Using whip stitch, sew the wings to the
sides of the body, following photograph
for position.

Embroider as follows:

The face: for each eye, using black tapestry
wool and backstitch, embroider an oval with
a vertical line either side of the iris area. Fill
in the irises with satin stitch in blue and the
areas on either side with satin stitch in
white; for the mouth, using black and satin
stitch, embroider a smile. Cut a strand of yarn B
10in (25cm) long and thread into needle. Take
yarn through head above each eye to form two
antenna. See also page 124.

 A

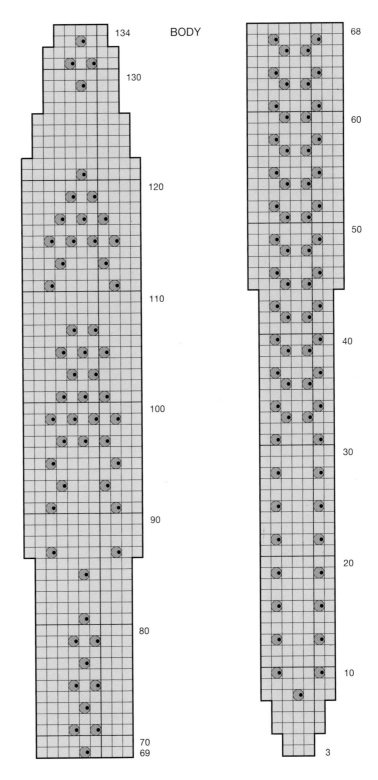

PB

You will find Titi Toadstool hanging out with Mimi Mushroom deep in the cardboard forest. They play hide-and-seek, but usually Titi gets found first as she can't keep quiet for long.

Titi Toadstool

pattern

FRONT

Legs
Using the thumb method and A, cast on 24 sts.
Row 1 (WS): Purl.
Row 2: K1, M1R, k10, M1R, k2, M1L, k10, M1L, k1. (28 sts)
Row 3: P1, M1L, p12, M1L, p2, M1R, p12, M1R, p1. (32 sts)
Row 4: K1, M1R, k14, M1R, k2, M1L, k14, M1L, k1. (36 sts)
Row 5: P17, M1L, p2, M1R, p17. (38 sts)
Row 6: K1, M1R, k17, M1R, k2, M1L, k17, M1L, k1. (42 sts)
Row 7: P20, M1L, p2, M1R, p20. (44 sts)
Row 8: K1, skpo, k18, M1R, k2, M1L, k18, k2tog, k1.
Row 9: P21, M1L, p2, M1R, p21. (46 sts)
Row 10: K1, skpo, k19, M1R, k2, M1L, k19, k2tog, k1.
Row 11: P1, p2tog, p19, M1L, p2, M1R, p19, p2togtbl, p1.
Row 12: As row 10.
Row 13: Bind (cast) (cast) off purlwise as follows: p2tog, p1, pass the first st loop on the right-hand needle over the second, cont to bind (cast) off 8 more sts, p23, bind (cast) off 9 sts, p2togtbl, pass the first st loop on the right-hand needle over the second. Fasten off. (24 sts)
Cut yarn.

Stalk
With RS facing, rejoin A.

Starting with a k row, work 24 rows st st.

Arms
Row 38: K1, M1R, k to last st, M1L, k1. (26 sts)
Row 39: P1, M1L, p to last st, M1R, p1. (28 sts)
Rep rows 38–39 once more. (32 sts)
Starting with a k row, work 2 rows st st.
Row 44: K1, skpo, k to last 3 sts, k2tog, k1. (30 sts)
Row 45: P1, p2tog, p to last 3 sts, p2togtbl, p1. (28 sts)
Rep rows 44–45 once more. (24 sts)
Starting with a k row, work 24 rows st st.

Cap
Join in B. Starting with a knit (RS) row, working in Fair Isle, stranding the yarn not in use on the WS and weaving in yarn as required, work color patt from the chart. Work shaping as follows:
Rows 72–81: Work 10 rows st st.
Cut yarns A and B.
Row 82: Using the thumb method and B, cast on 12 sts, work across row 82 of the chart, cast on 12 sts using the backward loop method. (48 sts)
Rows 83–99: Starting with a p row, work 17 rows st st.
Row 100: K1, skpo, k to last 3 sts, k2tog, k1. (46 sts)
Rows 101–105: Starting with a p row, work 5 rows st st.
Row 106: K1, skpo, k to last 3 sts, k2tog, k1. (44 sts)
Rows 107–109: Starting with a p row, work

Size
Completed creature measures approx. 14$^{1}/_{2}$in (36cm) tall

Yarn suggestion
Lightweight yarn (such as Debbie Bliss Rialto) 2 x 1$^{3}/_{4}$oz (50g) balls in A (white—23001) and 1 ball in B (red—23012)

Needles
Pair of US 5 (3.75mm) knitting needles

Other materials
Tapestry needle
Washable toy filling
Oddments of black, blue, and white tapestry wool for embroidery

Gauge (Tension)
24 sts and 38 rows to 4in (10cm) over st st using US 5 (3.75mm) needles

Abbreviations
See page 126

3 rows st st.

Rows 110–113: Rep rows 106–109 once. (42 sts)

Row 114: K1, skpo, k to last 3 sts, k2tog, k1. (40 sts)

Row 115: Purl.

Rows 116–119: Rep rows 114–115 twice. (36 sts)

Row 120: K1, skpo, k to last 3 sts, k2tog, k1. (34 sts)

Row 121: P1, p2tog, p to last 3 sts, p2togtbl, p1. (32 sts)

Rows 122–123: Rep rows 120–121 once. (28 sts)

Row 124: K1 [skpo] twice, k to last 5 sts, [k2tog] twice, k1. (24 sts)

Row 125: P1 [p2tog] twice, p to last 5 sts, [p2togtbl] twice, p1. (20 sts)

Row 126: K1 [skpo] twice, k to last 5 sts, [k2tog] twice, k1. (16 sts)

Row 127: Bind (cast) off 4 sts purlwise, p11. (12 sts)

Row 128: Bind (cast) off 4 sts knitwise, k7. (8 sts) Bind (cast) off.

BACK

Work as given for Front, reversing RS of work (to make a mirrored pair of pieces) by reading knit for purl and vice versa. See page 118 for reverse shaping tips.

FINISHING

Press pieces gently following directions on the yarn wrapper.

Using mattress stitch, sew the body pieces together around the outer edges, weaving loose ends into seam wherever possible, and leaving a small opening. Insert toy filling and sew opening closed.

Embroider as follows:

The face: for each eye, using black tapestry wool and backstitch, embroider an oval with a vertical line either side of the iris area. Fill in the irises with satin stitch in blue and the areas on either side with satin stitch in white; for the mouth, using black and satin stitch, embroider a smile on the lowest central white spot. See also page 124.

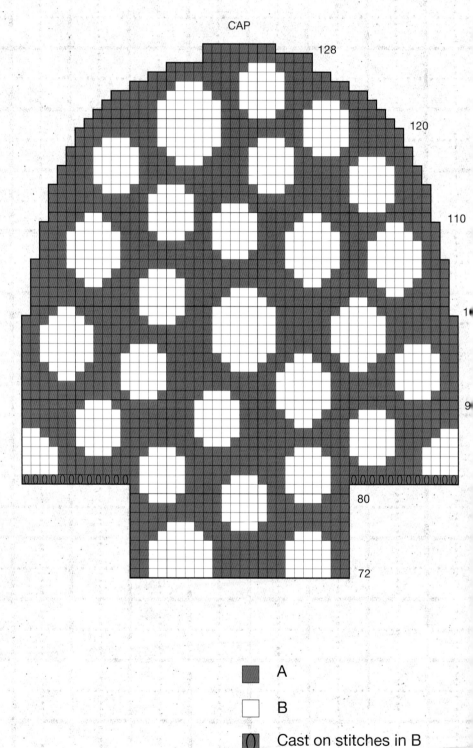

CAP

128

120

110

80

72

■ A

□ B

(0) Cast on stitches in B

Peggy Long Legs

Peggy has the longest legs ever, they just keep growing. She's about one yard tall and only five years old: imagine how tall she will be when she's 30! Peggy's favorite pastime is knitting and she's the fastest knitter in the world.

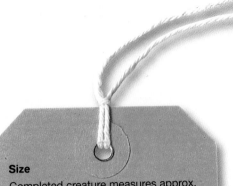

pattern

FRONT

Head

*Using US 6 (4mm) needles and the thumb method, cast on 24 sts.

Row 1 (WS): Purl.
Row 2: K1, M1R, k22, M1L, k1. (26 sts)
Row 3: Purl.
Row 4: K1, M1R, k24, M1L, k1. (28 sts)
Row 5: Purl.
Row 6: Knit.
Starting with a p row, work 5 rows st st.
Row 12: K1, skpo, k to last 3 sts, k2tog, k1. (26 sts)
Row 13: Purl.
Rep rows 12–13 four more times.
Starting with a k row, work 4 rows st st.

Shape arms

Row 26: Cast on 3 sts using the backward loop method, k to end. (21 sts)
Row 27: Cast on 3 sts using the backward loop method, p to end. (24 sts)
Row 28: K1, M1R, k to end. (25 sts)
Row 29: P1, M1L, p to end. (26 sts)
Row 30: K1, skpo, k to end. (25 sts)
Row 31: P1, p2tog, p to end. (24 sts)
Row 32: Bind (cast) off 3 sts, k to end. (21 sts)
Row 33: Bind (cast) off 3 sts, p to end. (18 sts)

Body

Starting with a k row, work 28 rows st st.
Row 62: K5, k2tog, k1, bind (cast) off 2 sts, skpo, k5. (7 sts on each needle)
Cut yarn* and put sts onto a stitch holder.

BACK

Starting with a new ball of yarn, work as given for Front from * to *, reversing RS of work (to make a mirrored pair of pieces) by reading knit for purl and vice versa. See page 118 for reverse shaping tips.

LEGS

Place Front and Back pieces WS together. Select one group of 7 sts on front and group of 7 sts opposite on back and put both groups of 7 sts onto two separate double-pointed needles. Put the remaining stitches of the other two groups of 7 sts onto a length of waste cotton yarn or two large safety pins.

First leg

**Join yarn to the outer edge.
Round 1: To start working in the round, use a third needle to k2tog, k3, use a fourth needle to k4, two from each of the original two needles. Use the needle that has now become free to k3, skpo. (4 sts on each needle.) Place round marker at the start of the round.
Knit 289 rounds.
Loop a short length of waste yarn through a stitch loop on the last round as a marker.**
Put all stitches onto a length of waste cotton yarn.
Do not cut yarn. **

Second leg

Put the remaining two groups of 7 sts on the stitch holders onto two separate double-pointed needles.
Rep as for First Leg from ** to **.

Both legs

Compare the amount of yarn rem in each ball of yarn.
Transferring stitches from waste yarn as necessary, cont to knit rounds on the leg with the least amount of yarn rem until 12in (30cm) of yarn rem.
Count the number of additional rounds from the marker on row 290.
***Next round:** [K2tog] six times. (6 sts)
Next round: Knit.
Cut yarn 4in (10cm) from the last stitch on the needle and thread into a tapestry needle. Pass the tapestry needle through all the stitches on the needles in the order they would have been knitted, use the tip of the needle to pull the yarn at the point just after it has passed through the first stitch to draw

Size

Completed creature measures approx. 50in (125cm) tall, including legs.

Yarn suggestion

Medium-weight yarn (such as Debbie Bliss Donegal Luxury Tweed) 2 x 1³/₄oz (50g) balls in A (pink—360001)

Needles

Pair of US 6 (4mm) knitting needles
Set of four double-pointed US 6 (4mm) knitting needles

Extras

Two stitch holders or large safety pins
Waste cotton yarn
Round marker
Tapestry needle
Washable toy filling
Oddments of black, green, white, and pale pink tapestry wool for embroidery

Gauge (Tension)

18 sts and 30 rows to 4in (10cm) over st st using US 6 (4mm) needles

Abbreviations

See page 126

the stitches tight to the yarn, then pull the yarn tight as it emerges through the last stitch. Secure the end. ***
Transfer stitches for other leg from waste yarn to needles.
Knit rounds equal to those of the additional rounds on the completed leg.
Rep from *** to ***.

FINISHING
Press pieces gently following directions on the yarn wrapper.
Note that the legs are not stuffed.
Using mattress stitch, sew body pieces together around the outer edges, weaving loose ends into seam wherever possible, and leaving a small opening. Insert toy filling and sew opening closed.
Embroider as follows:
The face: for each eye, using black tapestry wool and backstitch, embroider an oval with a vertical line either side of the iris area. Fill in the irises with satin stitch in green and the areas on either side with satin stitch in white; for the eyebrows, using black and backstitch, embroider a line above each eye; for the mouth, using black and backstitch, embroider an opening and outline the teeth. Fill in the teeth with satin stitch in white; for the cheeks, using satin stitch and pale pink, embroider circles either side of the mouth. See also page 124.

Knitting Equipment

Here are items of the basic equipment you will need to knit the creatures.

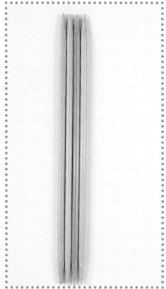

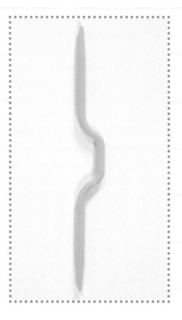

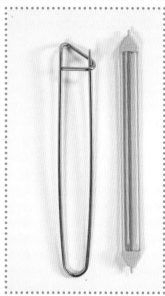

Above: knitting needles come in various sizes and materials; left to right, bamboo, metal, and plastic. Each pattern gives the size of the needles you need, but the type of needle is up to you. Beginners might find bamboo needles easiest to use as they aren't as smooth as the others so stitches don't tend to slip off unexpectedly.

Above: double-pointed knitting needles have a point at each end. This allows you to knit from either end and so knit in the round.

Above: the cable needle shown is a cranked one, which will hold the stitches safely while you work the cable.

Above: stitch holders are used to keep some stitches separate while you work on another part of the project.

Above: when you are working color knitting, wind lengths of the yarns onto separate bobbins and knit from these to avoid tangling up your balls of yarn.

Above: tapestry needles have a blunt point to help prevent them splitting the yarn when you are sewing up a project.

Above: there are various types of round marker, from metal rings to pretty, beaded ones. However, you can just use a loop of contrast-color yarn.

Knitting Techniques

If you are a novice knitter, these pages will show you how to get started so that you can knit the animals. Once you've mastered the basics, you'll also find instructions for more advanced techniques that feature in some of the creatures.

holding yarn and needles

There is no right or wrong way of holding the yarn and needles, so try these popular methods and use whichever feels most comfortable.

In the USA and UK the left-hand needle is usually held from above, like a knife, and the right-hand needle in the crook of your thumb, like a pen. The working end of the yarn (the end attached to the ball) goes over your right index finger, under your second finger and over your ring finger to help control the gauge (tension) of the stitches. Your right index finger moves back and forth to wind the yarn around the tip of the right-hand needle.

The other method, often called the "continental method", also holds the right-hand needle like a pen, but the left-hand needle is held between your thumb and second finger. The working yarn goes over your left index finger, under your second and ring fingers and over your little finger to control the gauge (tension). Your left index finger is held aloft and moves back and forth to wind the yarn around the tip of the right-hand needle.

slip knot

The starting point for any piece of knitting is a slip knot.

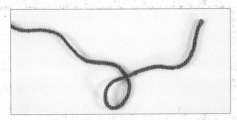

1 Lay the tail end of the yarn over the ball end to form a loop.

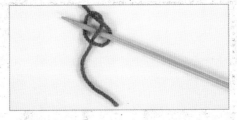

2 Bring the tail end under the ball end and across the back of the loop of yarn. Slip the tip of a knitting needle under this tail end.

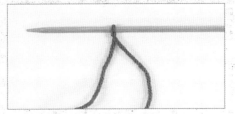

3 Pull on both ends of the yarn and the slip knot will tighten around the needle. This knot will always be the first cast on stitch.
After you have knitted the first couple of rows, you can pull gently on the tail end of the yarn to tighten the first stitch if it is a bit loose.

thumb cast on

This cast on involves using just one knitting needle and your left thumb and produces an elastic edge. If you are working with double-knitting yarn, making a slip knot about 20in (50cm) from the end will allow you to cast on about 40 stitches.

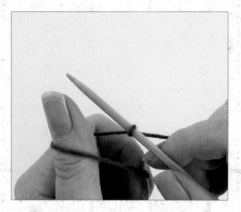

1 Make a slip knot the required distance from the end of the yarn. Hold the needle with the knot on in your right hand. *Wind the tail end of the yarn (the end not attached to the ball) clockwise around your left thumb.

2 Put the tip of the needle under the front of the loop of yarn around your thumb.

3 With your right index finger, wind the ball end of the yarn around the tip of the needle, taking it between the needle and your thumb and then around to the front.

4 Bring the knitting needle, and the ball-end loop around it, through the loop of yarn on your thumb.

5 Slip the loop off your thumb. Pull gently on the tail end of the yarn to tighten the stitch.* You have cast on a second stitch.

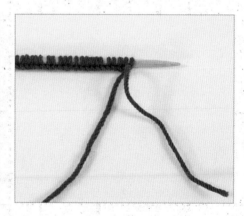

6 Repeat from * until you have cast on the required number of stitches onto the needle.

cable cast on

This method of casting on uses two knitting needles and produces a neat, firm edge. Always make the slip knot about 6in (15cm) from the end of the yarn to leave a tail long enough to weave in when the knitting is complete (see page 125).

1 Hold the needle with the knot on in your left hand. From left to right, put the tip of the right-hand needle into the front of the knot.

2 *Wind the ball end of the yarn around the tip of the right-hand needle, going under and then over the top of the needle.

3 Bring the right-hand knitting needle, and the loop of yarn wound around the tip of it, through the slip knot.

4 Slip the loop of yarn on the right-hand needle onto the left-hand needle. Pull gently on the ball end of the yarn to tighten the stitch. You have cast on a second stitch.

5 For all the following stitches, put the right-hand needle between the two previous stitches, instead of through the last stitch.

6 Repeat from * until you have cast on the required number of stitches onto the needle.

knit stitch

This is the first and most basic stitch you need to learn to start knitting, and it is very similar to the cable cast on (see page 113). First cast on the number of stitches needed for the project using whichever cast on method the pattern asks for.

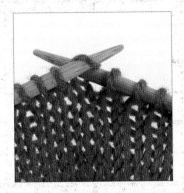   

1 *From left to right, put the tip of the right-hand needle into the front of the next stitch on the left-hand needle.

2 Wind the working yarn around the tip of the right-hand needle, going under and then over the top of the needle.

3 Bring the right-hand needle, and the loop of yarn around it, through the stitch on the left-hand needle.

4 Keeping the loop on the right-hand needle, slip the original stitch off the left-hand needle. You have knitted a stitch. Repeat from * until you have knitted all the stitches on the left-hand needle. Then swap the needles in your hands and you are ready to begin the next row.

purl stitch

This is the other basic stitch used in knitting.

1 *From right to left, put the tip of the right-hand needle into the front of the next stitch on the left-hand needle.

2 From front to back, wind the working yarn over the tip of the right-hand needle.

3 Bring the right-hand needle, and the loop of yarn around it, through the stitch on the left-hand needle.

4 Keeping the loop on the right-hand needle, slip the original stitch off the left-hand needle. You have purled a stitch. Repeat from * until you have purled all the stitches on the left-hand needle. Then swap the needles in your hands and you are ready to begin the next row.

binding (casting) off

This is the way you finish off your knitting, securing the stitches so that they don't unravel. It is shown here on a knit row, but can be worked just as well on a purl row: simply purl the stitches instead of knitting them.

1 Knit the first two stitches on the left-hand needle.

2 *Put the tip of the left-hand needle into the first stitch you knitted and lift it over the second stitch. Drop this first stitch off both needles.

3 Knit another stitch and repeat from * to bind (cast) off all the stitches in turn.

4 When you have just one stitch left on the right-hand needle, pull gently to open it up a little and slip it off the needle. Cut the yarn 6in (15cm) from the knitting. Thread the cut end through the last stitch and pull gently on the cut end to tighten the stitch.

knitting in the round

This is the technique used to work seamless tubes of knitting. It might seem fiddly at first, but do persevere as it isn't difficult once you get the hang of manipulating the four needles. An advantage of working in the round is that you only have to knit rows—there are no purl rows—to make stockinette (stocking) stitch. You can more or less ignore the needles that you are not actually knitting with.

The principles employed in holding two needles and yarn (see page 111) also apply when knitting in the round on four needles. Bring the lower end of the needle holding the stitches being worked over the top of the end of the needle below to it to allow you to knit easily. You can safely ignore the two other needles holding stitches: as long as the stitches are not too close to either end of the needle, they shouldn't fall off.

1 Cast on the required number of stitches using the appropriate cast on method (see pages 112–113) and double-pointed needles. Unless the pattern says otherwise, distribute the stitches evenly between three needles. To do this, slip one-third of them off one end of the needle onto a second needle. Slip another third of them off the other end of the needle onto a third needle. If you push the stitches to the middle of each needle they shouldn't fall off.

2 Before you join the stitches into the round, slip a stitch marker onto the free end of one needle. Make sure that the row of stitches is lying in a straight line across the three needles; not twisted at all. Put the fourth needle through the first stitch you cast on. Wrap the working end of the yarn firmly around the tip of the fourth needle and knit the stitch, pulling it tight so that the three needles with stitches on form a triangle.

3 Continue knitting the stitches on the first needle. When they are all knitted, then that needle is free and becomes the spare needle with which you can knit the stitches on the second needle.

4 Just keep knitting the stitches off each needle in turn to create a knitted tube. When you reach the stitch marker, slip it onto the next needle so that you always know where the beginning of the round is. Knit the first stitch on each needle firmly, pulling the yarn tight, to prevent gaps appearing in the knitting where the needles "join." If they do start to appear, then knit one stitch off the next needle for a round to change the position of the "joins."

gauge (tension)

The patterns in this book all specify the yarn you should use to knit them and the gauge (tension) the project requires. This is the number of stitches and rows there are in 4 x 4in (10 x 10cm) of knitted fabric. It is important that you work to the gauge (tension) the pattern states or the knitted fabric will be too baggy (if your gauge/tension is too loose), or too firm (if your gauge/tension is too tight). This might not sound dreadful, but it will affect the way your project looks, and if your gauge (tension) is too loose, you will use more yarn and may run out before finishing the knitting. So do take the time to knit a gauge (tension) swatch before starting to make your favorite character.

knitting a gauge (tension) swatch

First, find the gauge (tension) information given in the pattern. It will say something like: "22 stitches and 28 rows to 4in (10cm) over st st using US 6 (4mm) needles." What this means it that, using the stated yarn and needles and working in the specified stitch pattern, in a piece of knitting 4in (10cm) by 4in (10cm) you must have 22 stitches in one direction and 28 rows in the other direction.

So, using the right yarn and needles, cast on the number of stitches stated, plus ten. Knit the number of rows stated—in the stitch pattern specified—plus ten, then bind (cast) off. Make the bind (cast) off as loose as you can to avoid pulling in the top edge of the knitting.

measuring your gauge (tension)

The next step is to accurately measure your gauge (tension). Do this a few stitches or rows in from the edges as the cast-on and bound(cast)-off edges and the row ends can be tighter or looser than the stitches in the middle of the knitting, which are the ones that you must count.

Lay the swatch flat without stretching it. To count the number of stitches, lay a ruler across the swatch so that 4in (10cm) is measured out a few stitches in from either edge. Put a knitter's pin into the swatch at either end of the measured distance. Remove the ruler and count the number of stitches between the pins.

To count the number of rows, repeat the process, but lay the ruler vertically on the swatch so that 4in (10cm) is measured out a few rows from either edge.

altering your gauge (tension)

If you have the same numbers of stitches and rows as stated in the pattern, then you have the correct gauge (tension). You can go ahead and knit the project that you have chosen.

However, if you do not have the right numbers of stitches and rows, you need to alter your gauge (tension). Do not do this by trying to knit more tightly or loosely. Everyone has a "natural" gauge (tension), the gauge (tension) they automatically knit to, and if you try to knit to a different gauge (tension) your stitches will be uneven. Also, you will usually forget that you are trying to knit more tightly and your natural gauge (tension) will reassert itself, then you are back to square one.

The way to alter your gauge (tension) is to change the size of the knitting needles you are using. If you have too few stitches and rows, knit the swatch again using needles one size smaller. So, if the pattern asks for US (5mm) needles, try again using US 7 (4.5mm) needles. If you have too many stitches and rows, then try again with needles one size larger: US 9 (5.5mm) needles instead of US 8 (5mm). This may sound time-consuming and frustrating, but it's much better to knit a little square a few times than to spend more time and effort knitting a whole project that doesn't look right.

measuring stitches

measuring rows

increases

Increasing is making extra stitches in a row to make the knitting wider or to shape it.

make one (M1) This method involves creating a brand new stitch between two existing ones. It is almost completely invisible in the finished knitting.

1 Knit to the position of the increase. Using the tip of the left-hand needle, pick up the loop of yarn lying between the next two stitches. Pick it up by putting the tip of the needle through the front of the loop.

2 Knit into the back of the picked-up loop on the left-hand needle, then drop the loop.
You have created a completely new stitch and so increased by one stitch. The principle is exactly the same on a purl row.

increase (inc) This method involves knitting twice into a stitch. The increase is visible in the finished knitting as the second stitch made—which will lie to the right of the original stitch— has a small bar of yarn across the bottom of it.

1 Knit to the position of the increase. Knit into the next stitch in the usual way (see page 114), but do not drop the original stitch off the left-hand needle.

2 Now knit into the back of the same stitch on the left-hand needle, then drop it off the needle. You have made two stitches out of one and so increased by one stitch. The principle is exactly the same on a purl row.

make one left and right

You will find that some projects in this book specify "M1L" (make one left) and "M1R" (make one right). This is because, depending on which method you use, the made stitch slopes to the right or to the left. The technique shown here is "M1L." To work "M1R", pick up the strand between the two stitches by putting the tip of the left-hand needle through the back of the loop. Then knit into the front of the picked-up loop. If the project simply specifies "M1", then you can use whichever of the two methods of making a stitch that you find easiest.

reverse shaping

When reverse shaping, it is important to use the knit or purl increase or decrease that will follow the direction in which the shape of the creature is developing. On shaping rows, reverse the stitch (knit for purl or vice versa) and then use the table below to check which increase or decrease should be used at the beginning and end of the row to achieve a smooth effect. The direction the stitches slope in is given as though you are looking at them from the knit side of the work.

Knit increase

Beginning of row	End of row
MIR (right slanting)	M1L (left slanting)

Knit decrease

Beginning of row	End of row
skpo (left slanting)	k2tog (right slanting)

Purl increase

Beginning of row	End of row
MIL (left slanting)	M1R (right slanting)

Purl decrease

Beginning of row	End of row
p2tog (right slanting)	p2togtbl (left slanting)

decreases

Decreasing involves taking away stitches in a row to make the knitting narrower. Decreases slant in different directions, so when used at either end of a row, they mirror each other.

knit two together (k2tog) In this method you knit two stitches together to make one. The decrease slants to the right on a knit row.

purl two together (p2tog) This uses the same principle as k2tog to decrease stitches on a purl row. The decrease slants to the left on a purl row.

Knit to the position of the decrease. From left to right, put the tip of the right-hand needle through the front of the second stitch from the end of the left-hand needle, then through the first one. Knit the two stitches together in the usual way, just as if they were one.
You have made two stitches into one and so decreased by one stitch.

Purl to the position of the decrease. From right to left, put the tip of the right-hand needle through the next two stitches on the left-hand needle. Purl the two stitches together in the usual way, just as if they were one.
You have made two stitches into one and so decreased by one stitch.

slip one, knit one pass slipped stitch over (skpo) This method involves slipping a stitch and then passing the next one over it, rather like binding (casting) off. This decrease slants to the left on a knit row.

1 Knit to the position of the decrease. Put the right-hand needle into the next stitch, as if you were going to knit it, but slip it from the left-hand to the right-hand needle without knitting it.

2 Knit the next stitch on the left-hand needle in the usual way.

3 Put the tip of the left-hand needle into the slipped stitch and lift it over the knitted stitch, then drop it off both needles.
You have decreased by one stitch.

through the back loop (tbl)

Knitting or purling a stitch through the back of the loop (rather than through the front as normal), twists the stitch. This is used mainly in shaping to change the direction an increase or decrease slants in. For example, "k2togtbl" means knit two together (see page 119), but through the back loops.

To knit a stitch through the back loop, put the right-hand needle from right to left through the stitch, but putting it behind the left-hand needle. Take the yarn around the tip of the right-hand needle in the usual way and knit the stitch.

To purl a stitch through the back loop, put the right-hand needle from left to right through the back of the stitch: when you straighten the left-hand needle the stitch will be twisted around it, as shown. Take the yarn around the tip of the right-hand needle in the usual way and purl the stitch.

slipping stitches

Slipped stitches can be worked knitwise or purlwise. If the pattern does not specify which way to slip a stitch, slip it knitwise on a knit row, and purlwise on a purl row.

pick up and knit

Use this technique to start knitting from the edge of a piece that has been bound off. The knitting pattern will tell you how many stitches to pick up from where.

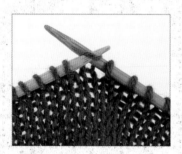

1 On a knit row, slip a stitch knitwise by putting the right-hand needle into the next stitch, as if to knit it, but slip it onto the needle without actually knitting it. Knit the next stitch in the usual way.

2 The principle is the same if you are slipping a stitch purlwise. Put the right-hand needle into the next stitch, as if to purl it, but slip it onto the needle without actually purling it. Purl the next stitch in the usual way.

1 Hold the yarn with which you are going to pick up the new stitches at the back of the finished piece. Put a knitting needle through the middle of the stitch to be picked up from. At the back, loop the yarn over the tip of the needle.

2 Bring the needle back through the stitch, bringing the loop of yarn through with it. You have picked up one stitch.

short-rowing

This is a technique for creating curved pieces of knitting. Each row will tell you to knit a number of stitches, then "short-row-wrap the next st, turn." Follow these wrapping techniques to wrap the next stitch in the row, then turn the knitting by swapping the needles in your hands.

on a knit row Knit the number of stitches stated then wrap the next stitch as follows.

1 Slip the next stitch on the left-hand needle purlwise onto the right-hand needle (see page 120).

2 Bring the yarn forward between the tips of the needles.

3 Now slip the stitch back onto the left-hand needle, then take the yarn to the back again, thus wrapping it around the slipped stitch. Here, the yarn is shown as a loop so that you can see what is happening, but you must pull it taut. Now you are ready to turn the work and purl the next row.

on a purl row Purl the number of stitches stated then wrap the next stitch as follows.

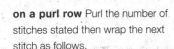

1 Slip the next stitch on the left-hand needle purlwise onto the right-hand needle (see page 120).

2 Take the yarn back between the tips of the needles.

3 Now slip the stitch back onto the left-hand needle, then bring the yarn to the front between the needles again, thus wrapping it around the slipped stitch. Now you are ready to turn the work and knit the next row.

picking up wraps on a knit row
Once the shaping rows are completed, you will knit or purl across all the stitches in the row. When doing this it is essential to work the wrap loops together with the slipped stitches they encircle to prevent holes forming. Follow the technique shown on each wrapped stitch as you get to it.

From the front and using the tip of the right-hand needle, pick up the wrap loop around the base of the slipped stitch. Slip this loop onto the tip of the left-hand needle and then knit the loop and stitch together as if they were one. The loop will not be visible on the right side of the work.

picking up wraps on a purl row
Working across the knitting on a purl row, follow the technique shown on each wrapped stitch as you get to it.

From behind and using the tip of the right-hand needle, pick up the wrap loop around the base of the slipped stitch. Slip this loop onto the tip of the left-hand needle then purl the loop and stitch together as one. The loop will not be visible on the right side of the work.

color knitting

There are two main techniques for color knitting, Fair Isle and intarsia. For both techniques it is important to twist the yarns around one another as shown to prevent holes appearing between the different-colored yarns. Whether colors change in straight lines or on the diagonal will, of course, depend on the motif you are knitting. Shown here are the principles of making all the color changes.

fair isle This method strands yarn across the back of the work and is used to knit continuous patterns. When using this technique, do not pull the yarn tight across the back of the work or it will pucker up. However, stranding it too loosely will result in loops on the back and baggy stitches, so practice the technique to get the balance right before starting a project.

1 On a knit row, knit to the first color change. Bring the new color yarn (purple) from under the original color yarn (pink), and then around the needle to knit the stitch.

2 Knit the stitches in the new color yarn. When you get to the next color change, bring that yarn (pink) from under the new color yarn (purple), and around the needle to knit the stitch.

3 If the interval between color changes is more than three stitches, you will need to weave the yarn not in use into the back of a stitch to prevent long loops forming on the back. Bring the working yarn under the yarn not in use, then knit the next stitch in the working yarn. Here the purple yarn is being woven in to the back of a pink stitch.

4 On a purl row, purl to the first color change. Bring the new color yarn (purple) under the original color (pink), and then around the needle to purl the stitch.

5 At the next color change, bring the original yarn (here it is pink) over the new yarn (purple), and purl the stitch.

6 If the interval between color changes is more than three stitches you must also weave in the yarn not in use on purl rows. Use the same procedure as for knit rows.

Above: where the yarn not in use is woven into the back of a stitch it may well show a little on the front, either as a slight pucker in the stitch or as a spot of color between stitches. This is inherent in Fair Isle knitting.

intarsia This method uses a separate ball of yarn for each colored area. To avoid tangling the yarns, wind long lengths onto bobbins and knit from these.

1 On a knit row, knit to the first color change. Bring the new color yarn (magenta) over the original color yarn (blue), and then around the needle to knit the stitch.

2 Knit the stitches in the new color yarn. When you get to the next color change, bring that yarn (magenta) over the original color yarn (blue), and around the needle to knit the stitch. To knit the next stitch in blue on the row shown, bring the blue yarn over the magenta yarn: this is shown below on a purl row where it can be seen more easily.

3 On a purl row, purl to the first color change. Bring the new color yarn (magenta) under the original color yarn (blue), and then around the needle to purl the stitch.

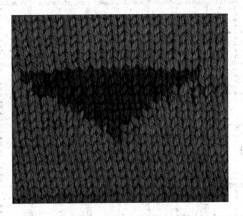

4 Purl the stitches in the new color yarn. When you get to the next color change, bring that yarn (magenta) under the original color yarn (blue), and around the needle to knit the stitch.

5 To work the next color change, bring the new color (now blue) over the old color (magenta) on both knit and purl rows.

Above: Weaving in ends neatly (see page 125) gives you the opportunity to tighten up any loose stitches at the beginning and end of an intarsia color motif.

cables

Cabling simply involves swapping the positions on the needle of groups of stitches. Shown here is cable four but you can cable two, six or eight stitches just as easily.

cable four back (C4B) A back cable twists to the right on the right side of the work.

1 Purl to the position of the cable. Take the yarn between the tips of the needles to the back of the work.

2 Slip the next two stitches on the left-hand knitting needle onto a cable needle.

3 With the cable needle at the back of the work, knit the next two stitches on the left-hand needle. Just ignore the cable needle while doing this.

4 Now knit the two stitches on the cable needle. Slide them to the end of the needle and knit them in the usual way. Purl to the end of the row, or to the next cable.

cable four front (C4F) A front (or "forward", as it is also known) cable twists to the left on the right side of the work. Work it in a similar way to a front cable, but leave the cable needle at the front of the work instead of at the back while you knit the next two stitches on the left-hand needle.

Left: this swatch of C4B is worked over eight rows; that is to say, the cable is twisted on every eighth row of knitting.

embroidering faces

This where you give your creature its personality. Each project tells you how the creature shown was embroidered, but you can change them as you wish.

For instance, Angry Ginger (page 54) looks angry because he has frowning eyebrows and spiky teeth, but you could make him happy or hopeful by turning his eyebrows the other way up and giving him a smile. After you have knitted and stuffed your creature, you are ready to embroider the face. You can use tapestry yarn in the colors you want, or use up any scraps of lightweight knitting yarn you might have lying around. Use a large embroidery needle with a big hole so you can thread your chosen yarn through it easily. The stitches and rows of the knitted fabric provide a natural grid, so it is easy to stitch onto.

Start by coming through from the back of the creature, guiding the needle to where you want the first eye to be on the front—you can snip off the tail of yarn later. Make a small backstitch to secure the yarn then backstitch the outline of the eye as if you were drawing it: I use a stitch about ¼in (5mm) long. After you have stitched the outline, fill in the whites and colored irises with satin stitch. Secure the yarn with a small backstitch, take it back through the creature and cut off the tail on the back. Embroider other features, such as mouths and cheeks, in the same way, outlining the shape first and then filling it in if necessary.

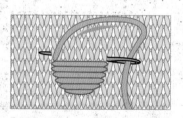

Satin stitch

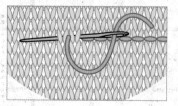

Backstitch

using a stitch holder

Some patterns tell you to place a certain number of stitches on a holder. You will work the remaining stitches on the knitting needles, then come back to the stitches on the holder and work those.

joining in new yarn

When you reach the end of a ball of yarn you need to join in a new one to continue knitting. You also use this method to join in a different-colored yarn in color knitting (see pages 122–123).

weaving in ends

When you have finished your knitting, you need to weave in any ends left dangling from casting on, casting off and joining in new yarn.

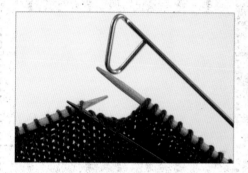

Simply slip the required number of stitches from the needle onto the holder. Make sure that the holder is securely closed, then ignore it until the pattern tells you otherwise. At that point, slip the stitches back onto the needle and work them as instructed.

If you are joining in new yarn because you have come to the end of a ball, join it in at the end of a row. You must have a length of yarn approximately four times the width of the knitting to knit one row.

Tie the new yarn in a loose single knot around the tail end of the old yarn. Slide the knot up to the work and pull it tight. Leave a 6in (15cm) tail of each yarn to weave in later.

Thread a knitter's sewing needle with the tail of yarn. Take the needle back and forth, not in and over, through the backs of several stitches. Go through approximately four stitches in one direction, then work back through the last two again. If you are weaving in ends from color knitting, weave the tails into stitches of the same color to stop them showing on the front.

blocking

Once you have finished your knitting project, it will benefit from being blocked. This smooths out the fabric, helps hide any small imperfections and makes the project much easier to sew up.

On an ironing board, lay out your project pieces without stretching them. Ease each piece to the correct size and shape. Pin the pieces to the board by pushing dressmaker's pins through the edge stitches into the board.
Carefully following the instructions on the yarn yarn wrapper, press all the pieces. Leave

them pinned out until they are completely cold. Then take out all the pins and you are ready to start sewing up your project.

sewing up

Many people rush this stage of making a knitting project, which is a mistake. Take your time, use mattress stitch as shown here, and your seams will be smooth and neat, giving your knitting a professional finish. Use the yarn you used to knit the project to sew it up, though if the yarn is very fine or breaks easily, use a stronger one in the same fiber and color.

 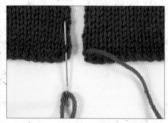  

1 Thread a knitter's sewing needle with a long length of yarn. Here, a contrast color has been used for clarity. Secure the yarn on the back of one of the pieces to be joined by taking it over a couple of stitches, a couple of times. Bring the needle to the front of the fabric, bringing it up between the first two stitches on the first row.

2 Right-side up, lay the other project piece to be joined next to the first piece. From the front, take the needle through the fabric between the first two stitches on the first row and up under the bars of two stitches. Pull the yarn through.

3 Take the needle back through where it came out on the first piece and up under the bars of two stitches. Take the needle back to the other piece, through where it came out and up under the bars of two stitches. Zigzag between the pieces, taking the needle under two stitch bars each time. Gently pull the yarn to close the seam as you work.

Above: worked neatly a mattress stitched seam blends in to the knitted fabric.

abbreviations

Here is a list of the abbreviations you will find in the knitting patterns in this book.

A, B, C, etc	colors as indicated in the pattern	**double-inc**	knit into the front, back and front again of the same stitch	**p**	purl	**skpo**	slip one, knit one, pass slipped stitch over
alt	alternate	**back**		**patt(s)**	pattern(s)	**sl**	slip
approx	approximate	**dpn**	double-pointed needle(s)	**PB**	place bead	**st(s)**	stitch(es)
beg	begin, beginning, begins	**g**	gram(s)	**psso**	pass slipped stitch over	**st st**	stockinette stitch
C4B	cable four (or number stated) back	**inc(s)**	increase, increasing, increases	**rem**	remain, remaining	**tbl**	through the back loop
				rep(s)	repeat(s)	**tog**	together
C4F	cable four (or number stated) forward	**k2tog**	knit two together	**rev st st**	reverse stockinette stitch	**WS**	wrong side
		k	knit	**RS**	right side	*****	repeat instructions between/following * as many times as instructed
cm	centimeter(s)	**mm**	millimeters	**s2tog, k1, psso**	slip next two stitches together knitwise (put needle into second then first stitch to do this), knit next stitch, pass slipped stitches over knitted stitch		
cont	continue	**M1**	make one stitch				
dec(s)	decrease, decreasing, decreases	**M1L**	make one stitch left			**[ ]**	repeat instructions between [ ] as many times as instructed
		M1R	make one stitch right				
DK	double knitting	**oz**	ounce(s)				
		p2tog	purl two together				

yarn information

Here is the weight, yardage, and fiber content for all the yarns used in this book.

Debbie Bliss Baby Cashmerino
Sport
1¾oz/50g; 137yds/125m;
55% merino wool, 33% microfibre,
12% cashmere.

Debbie Bliss Cashmerino DK
Light worsted (DK)
1¾oz/50g; 120yds/110m;
55% merino wool, 33% mircofibre,
12% cashmere.

**Debbie Bliss Donegal
Luxury Tweed**
Worsted (Aran)
1¾oz/50g; 96yds/88m;
85% wool, 15% angora.

Debbie Bliss Prima
Light worsted (DK)
1¾oz/50g; 109yds/100m;
80% bamboo, 20% merino wool.

Debbie Bliss Rialto
Light worsted (DK)
1¾oz/50g; 115yds/105m;
100% extra fine merino wool.

Lang Yarns West
Super bulky (super chunky)
1¾oz/50g; 100yds/92m;
55% new wool, 45% acrylic.

Lion Brand Cotton-Ease
Worsted (Aran)
3½oz/100g; 207yds/188m;
50% cotton, 50% acrylic.

Lion Brand Fishermen's Wool
Worsted (Aran)
8oz/227g; 465yds/425m;
100% pure virgin wool.

Lion Brand Sock-Ease
Fingering (4-ply)
3½oz/100g; 438yds/400m;
75% wool, 25% nylon.

**Lion Brand Vanna's
Choice Baby**
Worsted (Aran)
3½oz/100g; 170yds/156m;
100% acrylic.

Rowan 4-ply Soft
Fingering (4-ply)
1¾oz/50g; 191yds/175m;
100% merino wool.

Rowan All Seasons Cotton
Light worsted (DK)
1¾oz/50g; 98yds/90m;
60% cotton, 40% acrylic/
microfiber.

Rowan Cashcotton 4-ply
Fingering (4-ply)
1¾oz/50g; 197yds/180m;
35% cotton, 25% polyamide,
18% viscose, 9% cashmere.

Rowan Cotton Glacé
Light worsted (DK)
1¾oz/50g; 126yds/115m;
100% cotton.

Rowan Kid Classic
Worsted (Aran)
1¾oz/50g; 153yds/140m;
70% lambswool, 26% mohair,
4% nylon.

Rowan Kidsilk Haze
Lace (2-ply)
1oz/25g; 230yds/210m;
70% super kid mohair, 30% silk.

Rowan Pure Wool 4-ply
Fingering (4-ply)
1¾oz/50g; 175yds/160m;
100% super wash wool.

Rowan Pure Wool DK
Light worsted (DK)
1¾oz/50g; 137yds/125m;
100% super wash wool,

Rowan Scottish Tweed 4-ply
Fingering (4-ply)
1oz/25g; 120yds/110m;
100% pure new wool.

Rowan Wool Cotton
Light worsted (DK)
1¾oz/50g; 123yds/113m;
50% merino wool, 50% cotton.

Sublime Angora Merino
Light worsted (DK)
1¾oz/50g; 131yds/120m;
80% extra fine merino wool,
20% angora.

**Sublime Cashmere Merino
Silk DK**
Light worsted (DK)
1¾oz/50g; 127yds/116m;
75% extra fine merino wool,
20% silk, 5% cashmere.

**Twilley's Washable
Goldfingering**
Lace (2-ply)
1oz/25g; 104yds/95m;
80% viscose, 20% polyester.

substituting yarn

If you decide to use a yarn that is different to the one suggested, follow these simple rules before buying.

Firstly, unless you are an experienced knitter do use a yarn that is the suggested weight. If you use a sport-weight where the project asks for a bulky (chunky) weight, you may have problems with some of the patterns. Secondly, it is the number of yards (yds) or meters (m) of yarn in each ball, not the weight of the ball, that is important. Balls of different brands of yarn, even if they are the same weight, will not necessarily contain the same number of yds/m of yarn. So you cannot just buy the number of balls the pattern asks for in your substitute yarn: you need to do two sums, but they are simple ones. Given on the left are the number of yds/m per ball for the yarns used in the projects. Multiply the appropriate number of yds/m by the number of balls needed to knit the project. This will give you the total number of yds/m of yarn you will need. Now check the yarn wrapper of your substitute yarn to see how many yds/m there are in a ball. Divide the total number of yds/m needed by the number in one ball of the substitute yarn and this will tell you how many balls of that yarn you need to buy.
Before you start knitting the project, you absolutely must knit a gauge (tension) swatch in the substitute yarn to check that it will achieve the gauge (tension) stated in the pattern.

Resources

Donna Wilson can be contacted at info@donnawilson.com. Visit her website at donnawilson.com, find her on Facebook or on Twitter @DonnaWilsonLtd.

USA

Debbie Bliss yarns
Sublime yarns
Knitting Fever Inc.
P.O. Box 336
315 Bayview Ave.
Amityville, NY 11701
www.knittingfever.com

Lang Yarns
Berroco Inc.
1 Tupperware Dr., Suite 4
N. Smithfield, RI 0286-6815
Tel: 401-769-1212
www.berroco.com

Lion Brand Yarn
135 Kero Road
Carlstadt, NJ 07072
Tel: 800-661-7551
www.lionbrand.com

Rowan Yarns
Westminster Fibers
165 Ledge St
Nashua, NH 03060
Tel: 800-445-9276
www.westminsterfibers.com

Twilleys of Stamford
www.deramores.com/twilleys

CANADA

Debbie Bliss yarns
Rowan Yarns
Sublime
Diamond Yarns Ltd
155 Martin Ross Avenue
Unit 3
Toronto
Ontario M3J 2L9
www.diamondyarn.com

Lang Yarns
Estelle Design & Sales Limited
Unit 65
2220 Midland Avenue
Scarborough, Ontario M1P 3E6
Tel: 1 800 387 5167
www.estelledesigns.ca

Lion Brand Yarn
www.lionbrand.com for stockists

Twilleys of Stamford
www.deramores.com/twilleys

UK

Debbie Bliss yarns
Designer Yarns Ltd
Units 8–10
Newbridge Industrial Estate
Pitt Street
Keighley
West Yorkshire BD21 4PQ
Tel: 01535 664222
www.designeryarns.uk.com

Hobbycraft
Tel: 0330 026 1400
www.hobbycraft.co.uk

John Lewis
Tel: 0345 604 9049
www.johnlewis.com

Lang Yarns
Artyarn
10 High Street
Pointon
Sleaford
Lincolnshire NG34 0LX
Tel: 01529 240510
www.artyarn.co.uk

Lion Brand Yarn
www.banyantreeyarns.com

Rowan Yarns
Green Lane Mill
Holmfirth
West Yorkshire HD9 2DX
Tel: 01484 681881
www.knitrowan.com

Sublime
Tel: 01924 369666
www.sublimeyarns.com

Twilleys of Stamford
www.deramores.com/twilleys

Acknowledgments

I would like to thank Luise and Kate for being such amazing knitters and helping me interpret the creatures into hand knits so fantastically. Thanks to Tamar, Karin, Rachel, and Vanessa for their help and Jon for all his support. Thanks also to Cindy and the team at CICO Books for commissioning this book, to Luis for his creative book design and to Marilyn for diligent pattern checking. Rowan Yarns, Debbie Bliss, and Lion Brand were all very generous in supplying great yarns for the book.